A Clergy Guide to End-of-Life Issues

A Clergy Guide to End-of-Life Issues

Martha R. Jacobs

THE
PILGRIM
PRESS
Cleveland

This book is dedicated to my parents, who taught me the importance of caring for others and, by their example, showed me that with hard work I could achieve whatever I set my mind to and continued to love and accept me despite the barriers I sometimes set before them.

This book is also dedicated to my life partner of thirty years, Patricia A. Yost, who believed in me when I was unable to, saw in me the ability to teach, encouraged me to do the work that God had put before me, listened to the stories that I told about those whom I served, and, above all, helped me laugh after I cried for those who were suffering.

The Pilgrim Press
700 Prospect Avenue
Cleveland, Ohio 44115-1100
thepilgrimpress.com

© 2010 by Martha R. Jacobs.

All rights reserved. Published 2010

Printed in the United States of America on acid-free paper

Library of Congress Cataloging-in-Publication Data
Jacobs, Martha R., 1953–
    A clergy guide to end-of-life issues / Martha R. Jacobs.
      p. cm.
    Includes bibliographical references (p.   ).
    ISBN 978-0-8298-1859-8
    1. Death – Religious aspects – Christianity. 2. Terminally ill – Pastoral counseling of.
3. Church work with the terminally ill. I. Title.
    BV4338.J33 2010
    259′.4175 – dc22   2010000652

  4 5 6 7 8 9 10   20 19 18 17 16 15 14 13 12 11 10

Contents

Part One
END-OF-LIFE ISSUES

Part Two
THEOLOGICAL ISSUES

Part Three
PASTORAL ISSUES

Preface

This book is about the issues faced at the ending of life — the time before death when medical technology offers so many options and when families can be overwhelmed with grief and guilt. Almost 80 percent of medical costs in the United States are incurred during the last ninety days of life. This book is not about the cost side, but about the human emotion side. Medical plans have not been made by or discussed by many persons facing death. What if 80 percent of a person's faith resources, life philosophy, and fears also got summed up or "spent" during this time? What if the person facing death, family members, friends, and care providers could arrange for a fitting death as they all contemplate the loss during this final period?

During my eleven years as a hospital chaplain in medical centers and a community hospital, I became aware that many clergy have worked out caring programs for funerals, bereavement, even processes for funeral planning with those who are dying. Some ministers visit regularly and attend to family wishes. The hole in the donut is this: ministers frequently have not conversed with their congregants about health care desires as these persons have moved toward the end of their life. Okay, one can perhaps forgive delaying "the talk" when persons are in their thirties or forties. But Terri Schiavo was in her thirties when she entered a comatose state; the two women whose cases started the entire advance directives movement were in their twenties, so this topic needs to be discussed with anyone over the age of eighteen. Yet few of a minister's most frail congregants or those elderly living alone have been queried about their wishes.

From these experiences I embarked on a three-year journey to explore these questions and find a way to help both clergy and their congregants engage in the conversations that are often difficult but might have an immense healing impact on a person's last days, weeks, and maybe even months. I know there is a better way for clergy to facilitate end-of-life discussions and be more present with their congregants. I know that it is possible and vital, not only for the congregants and their families, but for the clergyperson as well.

While doing research, I came to understand that there are social, ethical, and racial implications regarding end-of-life decisions. There are trust issues: lack of trust in the medical system; lack of trust in doctors; lack of trust in other family members; lack of trust in one's own belief system. There are issues of denial for medical professionals, clergy, and individuals. There are political issues, which in some ways are actually religious issues that have been moved into the political arena, as witnessed by the Terri Schiavo case.

This book would not have been possible without the help of many people. While I cannot name them all, I do need to mention a few. My thanks go first to the Rev. Dr. Walter J. Smith, S.J., President and CEO of HealthCare Chaplaincy (HCC), for his support of my ministry and his guidance from my beginnings as a chaplain resident until now. To Jackson Kytle, Ph.D., for his support and encouragement and wisdom as I moved into writing this book, and to Helen Tannenbaum, the HCC librarian, who never tired of my asking for yet one more article. To my HCC and other chaplain colleagues, some of whose wisdom is included in the pages that follow, who provided input and were willing to take the time to help me figure out where I was going, particularly with the chapter on transformation. To the Hastings Center for their graciousness in allowing me to be a visiting scholar, taking over a desk in their wonderful library, and discussing around the lunch table (and in many side conversations) my wanderings and questions in areas that were new to some of the staff and had been contemplated by others for decades — issues about death and dying from a religious perspective. Particular thanks to my friend and colleague Nancy Berlinger, Ph.D., as well as Daniel Callahan, Ph.D., and Thomas Murray, Ph.D., for their time and wisdom. Sidney Callahan, Ph.D., was very helpful in figuring out transformation and how it affects both the individual and the community, and I am thankful for her time. My thanks to the students at New York Theological Seminary (NYTS), who raised questions and issues during my "Death is Not the Enemy" class and taught me as much as I taught them. To NYTS librarian, Professor Jerry Reisig, for his insights, particularly concerning transformation. To my Clinical Pastoral Education supervisors, particularly the Rev. Denise Haines, who taught me how to "be" and not "do" and showed me how to be present with those who were suffering; Denise also helped me connect my past with my future, for which I am most grateful. My thanks to Tarris Rosell, Ph.D., D.Min., at the Center for Practical Bioethics (CPB), for his encouragement and assistance with the materials on Compassion Sabbath. To my colleague and friend, Rev. Richard Sparrow, for his encouraging me to submit my dissertation to The Pilgrim Press and for his guidance with regard to helping local clergy deal with their own demons. To Scott Klares, M.D., for his reviewing the medical terminology to ensure that it at least made sense. To Rev. Timothy Staveteig for his willingness to take on this book and immeasurable help in shaping it and making it a doable project; to Joan Blake for her companionship on this journey through publishing; and to John Eagleson for his keen editing eye.

Without the willingness of those patients and families in the hospital who allowed me to be their chaplain at the most painful and difficult times of their lives, I would not have been able even to begin to write this book. Their loved one's death helped me to see that clergy need to do more to be present for their congregants who are dying and for their family members. I am so grateful to them and hope I have done justice to their experiences.

And last but certainly not least, my thanks to an awesome God who called me to serve despite my shortcomings, showed me the way, guided my thoughts and prayers, listened when I railed and questioned, and answered me with more grace and love than is humanly possible. Without God I would not have been able to do the work that I was called to do — serving those who are dying.

Chapter One

Why Are We Afraid to Die?

We often don't know what we don't know until we find ourselves in a situation that forces us into an area that is unknown to us or uncomfortable for us. One of these areas is helping congregants deal with end-of-life issues. In seminary, we learn how to do rituals that are required of us as clergy that cover the life-span of our congregants. We learn to deal with death by ensuring that people are "saved" before they die. We learn to do funerals, and we may learn how to do a memorial service. What we don't learn is how to deal with our mortality and with our actual dying. We do not have the opportunity to learn ministry for what I call a graceful death. Congregants need to know that their pastor is going to stay with them and that God is not going to desert them when they are dying. Congregants need guidance in making difficult decisions with regard to end-of-life issues. Family members need their pastor to be present when their loved one's life comes to an end. We need to provide a ministry that allows for a graceful death, that is, one where God's presence is felt. It is, therefore, a theological imperative as well as part of a ministry of compassion that compels us to learn how to help those whom we serve to have a graceful death.

I know there are clergy who do this very well, but based on my experience and that of many of my chaplain colleagues, many do not. I think there is an assumption that clergy "naturally" provide for a graceful death because we magically have the ability. After all, we are called by God to serve as God's representatives here on earth, so God provides us with those skills. But in reality many of the skills we learn as clergy we have been taught. Some are inherent, but just as there are those who are better preachers, so too there are those who are better at attending to the needs of their congregation when it comes to preparing for the end of life. This book will provide those who already have the ability to openly discuss death and dying with their congregation more tools and a deeper understanding of the legal issues involved with end of life; it will also give some additional insights into helping to facilitate a graceful death. And for those of you who get anxious and feel your stomach start to twist and turn at the thought of broaching this subject with your congregation let alone yourself or your family, this book will provide practical tools and guidance for your personal, professional, and spiritual growth with regard to end-of-life issues. For seminary students, it is my hope that this book will give you a foundational understanding of end-of-life issues and will also enable you to look at your own issues concerning death and dying so that you can put them aside in order to help someone achieve a graceful death.

During my years as a hospital chaplain, I became aware that many clergy had never conversed with their congregants about their health care wishes as they moved toward the end of their life (not even with their frail and elderly congregants, on those living alone). Some clergy had talked with individuals about how they wanted to be buried or what they wanted at their funeral, but clergy did not venture into discussions about what happens *before* someone's funeral.

As I watched patients and families struggle with issues that had never been discussed, and as I watched patients who were being kept "alive" by artificial means when there was no medical possibility that they would be restored to functioning on their own — hooked up to machinery that was only prolonging their inevitable death — I began to wonder why it is that we are so afraid to die. Why is it so difficult to accept that our bodies have a finite capacity to move and breathe and walk and talk? Why do so many clergy flee the bedside of the dying patient after performing a "drive by" prayer? Why is it that clergy don't want to talk about end-of-life issues any more than their congregants?

I know there is a better way for clergy to facilitate end-of-life discussions and be more present with their congregants. I know that it is possible and vital, not only for the congregants and their families, but for the clergyperson as well.

Clergy trained in dealing with end-of-life issues can then begin conversations with their congregants about their health care wishes. Congregants would then be better prepared with advance directives, or at least know to discuss their wishes with family members and, perhaps, with you, their clergyperson. They would then be empowered to have some input into their end-of-life health care.

The Importance of End-of-Life Issues for Clergy and Seminarians

End-of-life issues should have been addressed in seminary, before you were faced with them in ministry. Unfortunately, death and dying concerns were not a major part of my seminary education, nor are they part of most seminary course requirements. While I learned quite a bit during my Clinical Pastoral Education (CPE) units, I was not prepared to deal with some of the deeper theological and legal issues that surfaced once I was a professional chaplain. By teaching a seminary course entitled "Death Is Not the Enemy," my belief has been affirmed that seminarians need this training before they become pastors. The response from my students has been overwhelmingly positive. Some have been in the pulpit for years and decided to complete their formal education with a master of divinity degree. Their comments indicate that they wish they had known what they were now learning in class when they started out in ministry. They said that their life would have been a lot easier if they had not only understood the legal implications of death and dying, but had looked at their own issues and concerns regarding death and dying. One student mentioned talking with her pastor about what she was learning. To her surprise her pastor asked her to come back and teach what she was learning to other members of the clerical staff.

One of the outcomes of my research showed that, once ordained or out of seminary, clergy think that they know what they need to know. They do not know what they don't know and don't even know how to begin to ask the right questions of themselves let alone their congregants, particularly with regard to end-of-life concerns. I believe there is an unconscious agreement between clergy and their congregations to avoid discussions about issues of death and dying. In a Pew survey in February of 2006, the majority of people responded that their clergy did not talk about death and dying from the pulpit.[1] My own small survey confirms this findings.

So whose responsibility is it to talk about the things everyone wants to avoid? Whose responsibility is it to broach the subject thought by some as inappropriate for a sermon or a bible study? I believe it is our responsibility as clergy to learn to address these issues. It is also our responsibility to prepare tomorrow's leaders, and so these issues need to be part of the seminary curriculum.

Death is not the enemy, and yet we treat it as if it is. For those who have suffered greatly, physically, emotionally, mentally, or spiritually, death can be a release, a welcome "friend" who relieves us of our pain and suffering. For those who have not been present when someone dies, it is a mystery about which we would rather not know. For those who have been present when a loved one dies, it can be transforming not only for the person who has died, but also for the person who has witnessed the death. Death used to be a "natural" part of life. When clergy address, teach, and model these realities of our living and our dying, death can once again become a natural and much less frightening part of life.

This book, as well as the companion Internet website that supports it (*deathisnottheenemy.com*), in addition to providing clergy and seminarians with the nuts and bolts about end-of-life issues, will hopefully enable you to offer the ministry of a graceful death to congregants who are dying as well as to their family members. It will invite you to look inward as well as outward at death and dying.

Why We Are Afraid to Die

Then the LORD God said, "See, the man has become like one of us, knowing good and evil; and now, he might reach out his hand and take also from the tree of life, and eat, and live forever" — therefore the LORD God sent him forth from the Garden of Eden, to till the ground from which he was taken. He drove out the man; and at the east of the Garden of Eden he placed the cherubim, and a sword flaming and turning to guard the way to the tree of life. (Gen. 3:23–24)[2]

We were created with the intention that we would, someday, die. We may believe that the Bible is infallible and, therefore, the above passage is an affirmation that we will die, or we may believe that the Creation Story is exactly that — a story, a myth, written at a time and in a place where other Ancient Near Eastern religions had similar creation stories. However we look at the Bible, there is no interpretation that would lead us to believe that physically we were meant to live forever. Our physical bodies belie that. They are meant to break down, to wear out, to diminish, and to eventually succumb to disease, injury, or old age.

God has given us bodies that are meant to deteriorate over time. They are not made of unbreakable parts. There is a reason that our bodies can survive for only a limited period of time. To deny that we are mortal is, in a way, to deny God's creation. One of the powerful aspects of our faith is to trust in God, knowing that God will be with us as we live and as we die. As Christians we believe that our souls are going to be with God.

Our physical bodies will have done their work. There comes a time when we need to look at dying as a "transitional" way, a way that allows us to look to God for guidance and comfort and peace, knowing that God will desert neither us nor our loved ones. That is what faith is all about: to know that it is "well with my soul," as one hymn writer tells us.[3] To be well with our souls means to be in relationship with God and with Jesus and with our community. It means knowing deep down that God is not going to desert us in our time of need or deepest devastation. Just as I believe that God sighed with "sighs too deep for words" as his Son hung on the cross, I believe that God sighs with "sighs too deep for words" (Rom. 8:26) for us when we are suffering, whether that suffering be physical, spiritual, emotional, or psychological.

As Christians, while we may not know exactly what is on the other side of death, we do believe that God is there. So why do we need to deny death? Why do we want to live forever? Why do we try as hard as we can to outlive our bodies and their natural tendencies to wear out? Why is death an "enemy"?

The Denial of Death

Ernest Becker in his Pulitzer prize–winning book, *The Denial of Death,* addressed, in 1973, much of what we continue to wrestle with decades later. He was a cultural anthropologist, an interdisciplinary scientific thinker and writer who engaged theologians with death and dying issues in this groundbreaking book. He believed that he had found a very important principle for understanding human behavior and human culture, which he spells out in *The Denial of Death.*[4]

Becker asserted that human beings are vulnerable because we know we are mortal, and knowing that we are mortal gives rise to basic anxiety, even a terror about our situation. Therefore, we devise all sorts of strategies to escape awareness of and anxiety about our mortality and vulnerability. Becker claimed that this psychological denial of death is one of the most basic human drives in our individual behavior and is reflected throughout our culture. He believed that we spend our lives trying to create things that are immortal so that we will, through that "thing," become immortal ourselves. He thought that one of the most basic functions of culture is to help us avoid awareness of our mortality. Suppressing that awareness plays a crucial role in keeping us functioning. Imagine if we were constantly aware of our fragility, of the possibility that life could end any second: we would go crazy. Our culture helps us in this "denial" by making us feel that we are permanent, invulnerable, and eternal. In Becker's view, some of the consequences of this both socially and personally can be disastrous.

By ignoring our mortality and vulnerability we build up an unreal sense of ourselves, and we act out of a false sense of who and what we are. We set up what Becker calls "hero systems" (4). These systems are a part of us from the day we are born. We strive to be "heroes" within our cultures. Becker believes that it makes no difference "whether the cultural hero-system is frankly magical, religious, and primitive or secular, scientific and civilized" (5). People strive to be heroes "in order to earn a feeling of primary value, of cosmic specialness, of ultimate usefulness to creation, of unshakable meaning" (ibid.). It is intrinsically linked to our narcissism and helps to drive our ego toward the need to believe that we are immortal.

Becker believed that the denial of death pervades human culture. The notion of immortality pushes us to work to ensure that our lives have meaning, whereas death suggests that life adds up to nothing. People want desperately for their lives to mean something. So most of us try to ground our identities in something whose meaning seems permanent or enduring: our country, our nationality, our race, the arts or religions, or bricks and mortar. These cultural "icons" promise to connect our lives with what endures, with what does not perish, or what we perceive does not perish.

Becker acknowledged that there are people who do not avoid their mortality, people who do face up to the human situation. In most cases, it seems that the ones whom Becker cites as facing up to their human situation are those connected to religion. He mentioned Buddhism and quotes theologians such as Karl Barth, Paul Tillich, and Martin Luther.

Becker also wrote extensively about Søren Kierkegaard, who shared the belief that there are people who face the precariousness and fragility of existence: "One goes through it all to arrive at faith, the faith that one's very creatureliness has some meaning to a Creator;

that despite one's true insignificance, weakness, death, one's existence has meaning in some ultimate sense because it exists within an eternal and infinite scheme of things" (90).

Kierkegaard wrote about what he believed to be the basic formula of faith: "One is a creature who can do nothing, but one exists over against a living God for whom everything is possible.... Possibility leads nowhere if it does not lead to faith" (ibid.). Becker acknowledges that faith is the hardest thing (258), and then goes on to point out that Kierkegaard "placed himself between belief and faith, [and was] unable to make the jump" (ibid.)

Becker also quotes Luther's belief that you must be able to "taste death with the lips of your living body so that you can know emotionally that you are a creature who will die" (88). Further, he quotes Lutheran William James, who quoted Jacob Behem, who described this "tasting" of death as a "passage into nothing,... a passage in which a critical point must usually be passed, a corner turned within one" (ibid.). During this process of self-realization, the self is "brought down to nothing," which enables the process of "self-transcendence" to begin (89). Becker describes the process of self-transcendence this way:

> Man breaks through the bounds of merely cultural heroism; he destroys the character lie that had him perform as a hero in the everyday social scheme of things; and by doing so he opens himself up to infinity.... He links his secret inner self, his authentic talent, his deepest feelings of uniqueness ... to the very ground of creation. Out of the ruins of the broken cultural self there remains the mystery of the private, invisible, inner self which yearned for ultimate significance.... This invisible mystery at the heart of [the] creature now attains cosmic significance by affirming its connection with the invisible mystery at the heart of creation. (91)

"This," he concludes, "is the meaning of faith." Faith is the belief that despite one's "insignificance, weakness, death, one's existence has meaning in some ultimate sense because it exists within an eternal and infinite scheme of things brought about and maintained to some kind of design by some creative force" (ibid.).

Becker noted that Buddhism and many other faith traditions have faith in this sense. A faith that Becker characterizes as growing out of tasting one's own death, embracing one's own nothingness, and affirming an "invisible mystery" of ultimate meaning (ibid.).

In the final chapter of *Denial of Death*, Becker's seeking leads him back to Kierkegaard: "Faith is the hardest thing: he [Kierkegaard] placed himself between belief and faith, unable to make the jump. The jump doesn't depend on man after all — there's the rub: faith is a matter of grace" (ibid.).

Becker then quotes Paul Tillich: "Religion is first an open hand to receive gifts (grace) and then a closed hand to give them" (ibid.). Becker wrestles with looking at Kierkegaard's life as a believing Christian and places it against Freud's as an agnostic, and declares, "There is no balance sheet to draw" (ibid.). Yet he goes on to try to balance out the lives of the two men, coming to the conclusion that "in the game of life and death, no one stands taller than any other, unless it be a true saint, and only to conclude that sainthood itself is a matter of grace and not of human effort. My point is that for man not everything is possible" (259). His struggle continues with this question: "How does one lean on God and give over everything to Him and still stand on his own feet as a passionate human being?" (ibid.).

Becker finds William James a help in dealing with this ambiguity. James apparently understood how difficult it is to live in both the "visible" and the invisible worlds. Becker quotes one of James's precepts: "Son of man, stand upon your own feet so that I may speak with you" (ibid.), on which Becker comments, "If men lean too much on God they don't accomplish what they have to in this world on their own powers. In order to do anything one must first be a man, apart from anything else" (ibid.).

In *Denial of Death,* Becker is bringing into new light the nature of humanity. He is issuing a call to life and its living and to living with knowing that we will one day die.

As Daniel Callahan, bioethicist and philosopher, wrote: "Death is gradually being transformed from a fixed and unchangeable biological and human inevitability to a contingent event, even accidental and manipulable. Where death was once thought to be natural and therefore unchangeable, the very notion of 'the natural' is vanishing from our vocabulary, or at least from the vocabulary of aggressive medical research."[5] He lists the ways in which we currently die (death from disease, death from natural disasters, death from war and political upheavals, death from criminal violence, death from suicide, and death from accidents)[6] and wonders what will be in store for us as medical research gets more aggressive.[7]

Victory over death is an integral part of the Christian gospel. So as Christians we should be living our life knowing that death will come, but also knowing that we are responsible for our lives and for how we treat others as well as ourselves. Not living our life is denying that "every period is new, fresh, filled with its own hopes and carries within itself its own joys and sorrows."[8] Not living our life denies God and denies that God created us for some purpose, whether that purpose be to glorify God or to assist others in their lives. As Christians we should be able to overcome the fear of death. We should "celebrate the conquest not of physical death, but of the fear of death in life."[9]

A Graceful Death

In my work as a chaplain, I have spent many hours with patients who are "actively" dying. Both during my Clinical Pastoral Education (CPE) training and over time as a professional chaplain, I came to realize the importance to these patients of finding ways to express their feelings about their lives (both positive and not) and what life has been like for them. This led me to helping those who were dying to have a "graceful death."

With those who are able to communicate, I do a "life review." I ask them of what they are the proudest and what they wish they had done differently. I ask them to tell me about their life and its meaning for them. I ask how they hope to be remembered. These conversations are "holy ground" as I become a "witness" for the life that the person led. Most patients have some regrets about their life, but for the most part they also feel that they had done a "good job" and had worked to make a difference in this world. When we talk about their family members, I try to ensure that the family is present in the room so that they can hear what their loved one is saying about them. I also try to facilitate a discussion between the family and the patient so that the patient can hear what the family members gained from their life with the patient. (For a detailed use of life review, see chapter 6.)

For those who are not able to communicate, I invite the family to stand around the bed and ask them to tell me about the person: what they were like, how they lived their life, etc.

In helping people to realize that they would be remembered and that their life was not lived "for nothing," I was enabling exactly what Ernest Becker believed was so important for people: realizing that their life meant something, that at the time of their death they could look back and see that they were leaving something permanent and enduring. What the patients hear about is the love that they brought into our world through children, through relationships with significant others, through the way they lived their life and touched the lives of other people. This, to me, is a graceful death.

Helping people remember that God has been present and has been touched by the love that they have given to God's children also contributes to a graceful death.

Among my reasons for being present with families at the bedside, particularly when someone is dying, is to remind them that God is nearby, that God is also grieving the loss of one of God's creations. I have seen many people at their loved one's "death bed" come to a new understanding; that person has been healed.[10] I have talked with people who are dying who have come to a place of incredible peace because they have heard or felt "the Spirit of God," which has enlightened them, healed them, and released them from their sins and their fears and their worries. I have also talked with people who have not felt or heard "the Spirit of God" and are afraid that they will not hear it or feel it. And yet in talking about it, in claiming it, often they seem to have a "revelation" and come to a new and deeper understanding of the healing depth of God. This too is a graceful death.

I have felt blessed and incredibly graced when I have witnessed these healing "aha" moments. They are often quiet, still, but they are there. Is this true for all those whose deaths I have witnessed? No, but for a majority, when death comes, there is a peace that descends upon the body of the person. If one is still, one can sense God's presence. One can sense that holy moment when one of God's creations is reunited with God in a different way. This is the depth of God, a depth of which we can catch only a glimpse. This is a depth that we need to come to accept is in our best interest. I believe that this is the depth that Paul wrote about but could not really put into words. It is a depth we are aware of only in human terms, because "no eye has seen, nor ear heard, nor the human heart conceived what God has prepared for those who love him" (1 Cor. 2:9).

William Sloane Coffin wrote from a very different viewpoint in his book *Credo.* Coffin was aware that he was dying. His heart was giving out. He had lived with this condition far beyond when his doctors thought he would. He had a great deal of time to think about death and had some profound insights. Coffin writes, "Death cannot be the enemy if it's death that brings us to life. For just as without leave-taking there can be no arrival; without growing old there can be no growing up; without tears, no laughter; so without death there can be no living."[11] He goes on: "If our lives exemplify personal charity and the pursuit of social justice, then death will not be the enemy, but rather the friendly angel leading us on to the One whose highest hope is to be able to say to each and every one of us, 'Well done, thou good and faithful servant; enter into the joy of the Master.' "[12] This, ultimately, is a graceful death.

Why This Book Is Different

There have been many books on death and dying, but none have been specifically for Protestant clergy and seminarians. Other books have not offered a specific and pointed opportunity for clergy to deal with their own fears and concerns with regard to death and dying and how they can impact their work with their congregants, nor do they give clergy tools for use with those whom they serve. *The Last Dance: Encountering Death and Dying* (by Lynne Ann DeSpelder and Albert Lee Strickland) is a textbook used for college courses on death and dying, but not usually used in seminaries. *Life and Death Decisions: Psychological and Ethical Considerations in End-of-Life Care* (Phillip M. Kleespies) is geared toward psychologists and practitioners. Lastly, a small book entitled *A Good Death: Challenges, Choices, and Care Options* (Charles Meyers) is probably the closest in tone to my book, except that Meyers's book is not specifically directed to clergy and seminarians. Nor does it deal with a clergyperson's own issues that arise with death and dying.

As you are reading through this book, you might want to keep a journal of the feelings, thoughts, and ideas that come to the surface for you. This is meant to be a workbook, a book that makes you pause and think and consider the impact of not only your own life and death but the life and death of family members and those whom you serve. Death is a powerful part of our living. It is something that we all do. And whether or not we want to admit it, it is on our minds and in our hearts. So let's bring it out of the darkness of the unknown and expose it to the light of God, who is the Source of all.

Website Resources

Throughout this book, there will be references to materials or
links to various websites. While some of the URL addresses will
be included, particularly in the Appendices, you will also find
these links as well as the aforementioned materials on the website
www.deathisnottheenemy.com. You will be able to download documents for use with your congregations as well as several sermons to
give you some suggestions for your own sermons on death and dying.

Part One

End-of-Life Issues

Chapter Two

Legal Issues

An eighty-four-year-old man is brought into the emergency room by an ambulance. He had been unresponsive found by his caretaker. It is determined that he has had a stroke. This is the second stroke he has suffered. His old medical record was summoned and a health care agent form was found. His daughter-in-law, who had been designated as his agent,[1] was called, and she immediately came to the hospital. She told the emergency room doctor that after his first stroke, he told his family that he did not want to be kept alive if he suffered another stroke that was more debilitating than his first stroke, which had left him in a wheelchair and unable to take care of himself. After it was determined that he would not regain the ability to communicate, which had been the one function he had still been able to perform after his first stroke, the daughter-in-law informed the attending doctor that she did not want him hooked up to any machinery.

The doctor was not in agreement with the agent's decision and asked for an ethics consultation. As co-chair of the ethics committee, I talked with the daughter-in-law and read the proxy form. I then let the attending doctor know that he needed to follow the directions of the agent. He still disagreed and withdrew from the case. The patient's primary doctor was called, and he took over the care of the patient. The patient was moved to a private room and kept comfortable. What he was able to take in by mouth, he was given. He was not in any pain and for the most part rested comfortably. The family stayed with him around the clock. They read to him, talked about life together, and laughed and cried together. Their clergyperson came and anointed him and offered communion to the family, which they were grateful to receive. Their clergyperson and I kept in close contact, and we made sure that the family and the patient were tended to. Three days after his stroke, he stopped responding to his family, took in no nutrition, and appeared to be at peace, with no pain. Two days later, he died, with his family around him.

Another eighty-four-year-old person was brought into the emergency room about the same time, having suffered a series of small strokes. After several days, the doctor informed the family that their loved one would not be able to communicate with them. He would be confined to a wheelchair, having lost the ability to walk. The family was asked if there were any advance directives. They responded that they never wanted to talk about death with their loved one, so no, there were no advance directives. The patient was transferred to the intensive care unit (ICU). Eventually he had to be placed on a respirator because he could not breathe on his own. He was also provided with artificial nutrition and hydration. The patient was able to open his eyes but did not seem to know his family. Once he was stabilized, he was transported to a nursing home, where he lived for some time before succumbing to an infection. During this period, as chaplain I spent some time with the family, and their clergyperson came by from time to time as well.

One of the family members saw me in the hall one day, started crying, and told me how terrible things were for her dad. She said that he never would have wanted to be kept alive this way. I asked her how she knew that, and she said she "just knew." I explained to her that "just knowing" was not good enough in New York State because of the laws concerning advance directives. She asked how they could have avoided this situation, and so we began a conversation about advance directives. Before going home that night, she got copies of blank health care proxy forms and left swearing that everyone in the family was going to complete one because none of them wanted what had happened to her father to happen to them.

Advance Directives and How They Came About

Progress in medical technology has enabled doctors and other health care providers to sustain life for much longer than was ever previously anticipated. As this technology has developed, questions about how this technology can or should be used have increased. Among these issues are the drain on what might be scarce financial and spiritual resources for families and hospitals. What it comes down to is that the patient's interest is universally held to be sovereign.

There are those who believe that everything should be done to keep a person alive no matter what the possible outcome. Others believe that individuals should have the right to determine whether or not to be kept alive by technological means, for how long, and to what end. While the advancement of lifesaving machines and other technologies were initially intended to assist someone in the short term, this technology is now being used well beyond its initial intent. There is, moreover, a strong and ongoing debate about whether these heroic measures are in the best interest of the patient or were intended by God. In a conversation I had with a clergyperson about these issues, he put it this way: "We have idolized machinery. We worship machinery instead of praying to God to help us accept our impending death." Or as Margaret Mohrmann, theologian and medical doctor, writes, "[O]ur adoration of machines and high-tech procedures is a superficial issue and its elimination . . . would still leave intact the deeper idolatry that supports it, the idolatry of health and the idolatry of life."[2] She writes that our health is important and good "only insofar as it enables us to be the joyful, whole persons God has created us to be and to perform the service to our neighbors that God calls us to perform. . . . Health is to be sought in and for God, not instead of God."[3] And Daniel Callahan states: "constant clinical innovation has made it increasingly hard to know when someone is dying; the line between living and dying has become steadily more obscure."[4]

Many of the issues raised by modern technology involve deep theological questions for patients, family members, doctors, and hospital staff, as was manifest in the case of Terri Schiavo. It is important, therefore, that we understand why there are measures in place to help protect people. We also need to sort out our own feelings about these issues, so that we can better assist our congregants as they make their own decisions about end-of-life issues that involve artificial means of supporting life. (Chapter 5 includes a prayerful discernment process you can use to assist you in sorting out your own feelings.)

While the patient's interests are sovereign, just what these "interests" are is not so clear. They are as different as we are as people. So it is important to understand the history, the nuances of the laws, and the various states' positions on a patient's rights as well as denominational guidelines. With this knowledge we will have a better understanding of the implications for those whom we serve, and we can then empower them to make informed decisions about the sovereign rights to which they are entitled.

The Law

There have been several landmark rulings that have changed the end-of-life debate. The earliest was not about end of life itself. It was about the right of a person to say no to a physical examination. The Supreme Court in 1891 wrote:

> No right is held more sacred, or is more carefully guarded by the common law, than the right of every individual to the possession and control of his own person, free from all restraint or interference of others, unless by clear and unquestionable authority of law.[5]

Another very early judgment by the Supreme Court is attributable to U.S. Supreme Court Justice Benjamin Cardozo. In 1914, in *Schloendorff v. Society of New York Hospital,* he wrote, "every human being of adult years of sound mind has a right to determine what shall be done with his own body."[6] Judge Cardozo established the legal principle known as "informed consent," which declares that an adult citizen has a right to decide what happens to his or her own body. Consequently, a competent adult is entitled to determine what medical care he or she wishes to receive and doctors, nurses, and hospitals are bound to respect those care decisions. The concept of an advance medical directive is based on this first principle established by Judge Cardozo. The second equally important principle is that while citizens are in a state of competency and normal health, they can make decisions about what medical care they wish to have in the event they become incompetent (that is, they cannot communicate with medical-care providers).[7]

The right of a competent patient to refuse life-sustaining treatment was established in two cases.[8] The first was *Bartling v. Supreme Court* (1984), where the California Court of Appeals held that a patient could be removed from a mechanical ventilator at his request and over the objections of his physician and his hospital. The second was *Bouvia v. Supreme Court* (1986), again before the California Court of Appeals, which found that a conscious and competent hospitalized patient who was in severe and intractable pain could refuse nutrition and hydration with the understanding that it would hasten his death.

In addition to these two cases are the landmark Quinlan and Cruzan decisions and the much publicized debate about Terri Schiavo. Taken together, these cases helped to change and shape the way people consider life-sustaining machinery — machinery that might keep them alive for an indeterminate period of time, even without any significant improvement or consideration of a quality of life that is acceptable for that person.

In 1976, Karen Ann Quinlan's family took her case to the Supreme Court. Twenty-one-year-old Karen had stopped breathing after swallowing alcohol and tranquilizers at a party. Karen had been in a persistent vegetative state for several years and her parents wanted her removed from life support so that she could die. She was receiving artificial nutrition and hydration (feeding through tubes) and her breathing was almost fully supported by a mechanical respirator. The Supreme Court, In re *Quinlan,* ordered that the respirator be removed. The story goes that Karen was in a Catholic nursing home, and the Sisters had been weaning her from the respirator for some time, knowing that the court might rule that the respirator be removed. When the court issued its ruling, the respirator was removed and Karen was able to breathe on her own. She remained in this persistent vegetative state for another ten years before succumbing to pneumonia. There was never any discussion about removal of the feeding tube.

Then in the 1980s, a twenty-six-year-old woman, Nancy Beth Cruzan, was in a terrible car crash that left her in a persistent vegetative state. She also had no higher-brain function and was being kept alive only by a feeding tube and twenty-four-hour medical care. After several years, her parents went to court when the health care facility refused to remove the feeding tube. This case also went to the U.S. Supreme Court, which ruled that the wishes expressed by Nancy as to her medical treatment must be respected. The Supreme Court then sent the case back to the Missouri Supreme Court, which had the burden of ascertaining whether or not Nancy's parents had "clear and convincing evidence" of Nancy's wishes not to be kept alive by artificial means. The court was convinced and the feeding tube was removed in December of 1990. Nancy died shortly thereafter. (For more information on what constitutes "clear and convincing evidence," see "Other Legal Terms" below, page 30.)

Terri Schiavo was forty-one, resided in a nursing home in Florida, and had been determined to be in a persistent vegetative state in February of 1990, after suffering a cardiac arrest and a severe loss of oxygen to her brain. Her parents did not accept this diagnosis and believed that she responded to their voices and made purposeful movements. Her husband, who said that she had told him that she did not want to be kept alive if ever she was in such a state, petitioned to have the feeding tube that had been providing all "nutrients" to her, disconnected, so that she could die. Her parents fought against it and were able to rally members of the public, including some clergy, who vehemently opposed the removal of the feeding tube. They held vigils outside the nursing home and made life difficult for the nursing home and for Mr. Schiavo. He went to court on many occasions beginning in 2001, where judges sometimes ruled for and sometimes ruled against his request to have the feeding tube removed. In 2005, those who wanted the feeding tube to remain in place were able to involve the U.S. Senate and the president of the United States, who tried, in an unprecedented move, to intervene and stop the removal. Eventually, the U.S. Supreme Court refused to grant a stay and the feeding tube was removed. Terri died on March 31, 2005, two weeks after the feeding tube was removed. An autopsy revealed that, despite her parent's hopes to the contrary, her brain damage was severe. Schiavo's brain weighed about half what a healthy human brain weighs, and showed damage that left her unable to think, feel, see, or interact in any way with her environment. What this case showed is the extent of the passions that surround end-of-life decisions and highlight the need for people to complete advance directives.

How Different States Handle Advance Directives

To respond to the Supreme Court ruling in the Cruzan case, all fifty state legislatures had to provide statutory guidelines for some form of advance directives that would address the question of "clear and convincing evidence." Forty-six states and the District of Columbia chose to meet the Court's mandate through both living wills and the ability to appoint a health care agent, surrogate, or proxy. Alaska chose to recognize only living wills, whereas Massachusetts, Michigan, and New York chose to recognize only a health care agent.[9] More than thirty states created a law that lists family members and friends who are authorized to make decisions for a person who cannot make decisions for themselves. While it is not perfect — and families can still argue over what "mom would have wanted" — it is better than in the states where the person has no agent and is, therefore, in a kind of legal limbo, which then requires that "everything be done" because there is no agent.

The United States Congress responded by enacting the Patient Self-Determination Act (PSD). This legislation requires health care institutions at the time of admission to a hospital or nursing home to disseminate written information to patients about their rights under state law to refuse treatment and to prepare an advance directive.[10]

New York State, for example, drafted its law to enable someone to complete a two-page health care agent (HCP) form, naming another individual to make health care decisions only in the event that the patient cannot make them for himself or herself. Conversations about the potential patient's wishes are supposed to occur between the individual and the person who is named as the agent. This way, if decisions have to be made, the agent can know the wishes of the patient and follow through with them, whether or not the agent is in agreement with the person's wishes. The agent is to make decisions as if he or she were the patient, voicing the wishes of the patient.

California, on the other hand, has an eight-page form that allows you to select an agent, which could be your doctor (this is not allowed New York State), and includes sections similar to a living will.

In Texas, health care providers are allowed to determine that further life-extending treatment for a patient is futile and unilaterally decide — even against family wishes — that the treatment should be discontinued.

Each state is different. The information in Appendix 1 is current to 2010 (most states have not changed their laws in many years). To assure that you know about the laws of the state in which you are working, check the listings of online resources where you can educate yourself as to how best to assist your congregants.

There are those who believe that advance directive laws are not useful because most people do not know about them,[11] and recent studies indicate that people do not complete advance directives because of a lack of knowledge about advance directive.[12] Clergy are in a pivotal position and can make sure that their congregants are informed and empowered so that their health care wishes are honored. (In chapter 7, there are tools to help you to raise these issues with your congregants.)

So What Exactly Are Advance Directives?

An advance directive is usually a written statement made by a competent person about choices for medical treatment or selecting a substitute medical decision maker. The advance directive normally takes effect only if the person should become unable to make such decisions or communicate them at some time in the future. It makes our preferences known to health care providers and others who know us and care about us. The two most common forms of advance directives are health care proxies (or durable power of attorney for health care) and living wills. Do-not-resuscitate (DNR) orders are another form of advance directive that is written in the hospital or when under hospice care. Some states have developed do not resuscitate order forms that serve as advance directives because they are signed by both patient and physician.

Naming a Health Care Proxy

The health care proxy form allows an individual to appoint another person called the agent, proxy, or surrogate, to make health care decisions for the individual should that individual not be able to make decisions for himself or herself. As the individual's representative, that person is allowed to view medical records, sit in on care conferences and discuss medical treatment with all health care providers who are tending to the health care needs of that individual. The agent is expected to act in accordance with the wishes of the individual. Of course, this means that there have to have been conversations between the individual and the person being appointed as the agent. Some people have found out that they were appointed the agent only after the individual was already unable to communicate. This clearly is not helpful. Open discussions need to occur between the individual and the agent so that the agent can, with reasonable certainty, represent the wishes of the individual. These conversations should address at least the following questions:

- Is there a "bottom line" in terms of the quality of life that the individual wants to maintain in order for his or her life to have "meaning"?

- Does the individual want artificial nutrition and/or hydration extending life even if there is no reasonable expectation that the individual will have a quality of life that is acceptable to the individual?

- Does the individual want to be kept free from physical pain even if it means being unconscious?

- If the individual has permanent and severe brain injury and is not expected to recover, does he or she want to continue to be treated aggressively?

- If the individual is in a persistent vegetative state, does he or she want to continue to be maintained by artificial means (breathing, nutrition and hydration, antibiotics, etc.)?

- Does the individual want to be an organ donor? If so, are there any limits as to what can be donated?

In New York State, which has the highest standard of "clear and convincing evidence," agent statements about the conversation that took place between the individual and the agent are accepted when decisions to remove life support are discussed. However, if no discussion of artificial nutrition and/or hydration took place, it cannot be withheld or stopped once it is started. (New York has been debating this question for many years and the legislature has been considering changing the law to conform with the laws of other states, but to date, this has not happened.)

Most health care proxy forms require two witnesses who are witnessing that the form was not signed under "duress" and that the person named is capable of making this determination. The witnesses cannot be named as agent and do not need to know the details of conversations between the individual and the agent. Some states require a notary seal. The form will clearly state what the requirements are for it to be valid.

Living Wills

A living will specifies what the individual wants or does not want done in the event he or she becomes incapacitated or unable to participate in the discussions about his or her medical treatment decisions. It can be as specific or general as an individual wishes. One of the problems I have found with living wills is that they often do not cover everything that could happen to a person. For example, in at least two different cases in which I was involved, there were lengthy living wills that did not cover what actually happened to the individual, so an ethics consult had to be called and people had to try to figure out what the person would have wanted based on other criteria. Some living wills include an opportunity to appoint an agent or surrogate.

As I wrote in an article in *Plain Views,* the e-newsletter for which I am managing editor, I believe it is better to sign a health care proxy form than a living will.[13] I suggest that people appoint a health care agent, which enables the agent to make whatever decisions need to be made based on what is happening instead of letting the health care team and others who do not know the individual or his or her values make the decisions. Other experts also prefer a designation of an individual as the agent because "the person can actually represent your interests and interpret your choices in light of changing circumstances."[14] A living will "has to be interpreted by medical professionals, while an agent appointed in a medical power of attorney can make any and all decisions on your behalf."[15] Additionally, individuals who are present can be more flexible in exercising "judgment and [can] interpret the patient's wishes and values in light of specific and sometimes rapidly changing information about the patient's condition, treatment options, and prognosis."[16]

That being said, there are several different forms of living wills; some are listed in Appendix 3. Because a living will may be interpreted or used differently in different states, it is important to check your state's particular laws.

Do-Not-Resuscitate (DNR) Orders/ Do-Not-Intubate (DNI) Orders

A DNR order is a directive in the medical record that precludes the use of resuscitative measures such as chest compressions, artificial respiration, cardioversion, and/or cardioactive medications in the event of cardiopulmonary arrest — if a patient's heart stops or he or she stops breathing. In other words, a "code" is not called and attempts to resuscitate are not begun. A DNR order is issued by a physician and is written only when a patient is in the end stages of a terminal illness. It is initiated in the hospital or when a person goes into hospice. The patient or family member can request a DNR. If the primary physician does not want to issue a DNR (some will not issue a DNR for religious reasons), then that physician has to work with the patient and/or family to find another doctor who will take over the care of the patient and who will follow the wishes of the patient and/or family.

One of the misperceptions of a do-not-resuscitate order is that it means "do not treat." That is a fallacy. The patients continue to be bathed, fed (if capable), turned, given pain medications, receive dialysis, etc. The difference is that if their heart stops or they stop breathing, a "code" is not called.

Depending on the state, there can be several different DNR orders. If the patient has capacity, the patient can either verbally agree to a DNR or sign a form. If the patient does not have capacity, the agent can sign it. If there is no agent, a family member or close friend can sign it. In the absence of family or friends, two doctors can agree that it would not be in the patient's best interests (the patient would in all likelihood not survive the code).

Some states allow for a do-not-intubate (DNI) order. A DNI order means that a breathing tube will not be inserted down the throat if a patient experiences breathing difficulties or respiratory arrest. However, a "code" can be called and resuscitative measures such as chest compressions, cardioversion, and/or cardioactive medications may still be administered.

In some states (Texas, for example), a new term, Allow Natural Death (AND), is being utilized. This term describes more appropriately what is happening to the person who is dying. The natural trajectory of their illness is leading their heart to stop or their breathing to cease. It seems easier for loved ones to sign an Allow Natural Death instead of signing a paper that says "Do Not...."

Honoring Advance Directives

Because some hospitals and doctors do not follow the wishes of patients or their proxies, there has been a movement afoot to ensure that patient's wishes as expressed in advance directives are followed. The Physician Orders for Life-Sustaining Treatment (POLST) Paradigm Program "is designed to improve the quality of care people receive at the end of life. It is based on effective communication of patient wishes, documentation of medical orders on a brightly colored form, and a promise by health care professionals to honor these wishes."[17] There needs to be effective communication between the patient or legally designated decision-maker and health care professionals so that "decisions are sound and based on the patient's understanding their medical condition, their prognosis, the benefits and burdens of the life-sustaining treatment, and their personal goals for care."[18]

There is a POLST Task Force working to ensure that "seriously ill person's wishes regarding life-sustaining treatments are known, communicated, and honored across all health care settings."[19] On the POLST website, you can find which states are endorsing this program, which states are in process, and those that do not subscribe to the POLST program. See *www.ohsu.edu/polst/*.

Denominational Stances on Advance Directives and End-of-Life Issues

Most Protestant denominations have also weighed in on these difficult matters. In Appendix 2 and at *www.deathisnottheenemy.com* you will find information on those Protestant denominations that have taken an "official" stand on end-of-life issues.

Even with these official guidelines, individuals often seem to feel comfortable in doing what they believe is in their own best interest.

Other Legal Terms

There are several other legal terms that would be helpful for you to know about:

Capacity vs. Competence

"Competence" is a legal term. Whether or not someone is "competent" is determined by a judge. The judge determines whether or not one has basic cognitive and functional capacity to participate in decision-making.

"Capacity" is a medical term. Doctors (for example, physicians and psychiatrists) determine the extent to which one is able to understand the information concerning a treatment decision and appreciate the reasonably foreseeable consequences of a decision or lack of a decision.

When one has capacity, one can complete a health care proxy form, sign or consent to a DNR order, and/or make any and all other health care decisions. It should be noted that mental illness or a diagnosis of depression does not automatically render a patient "incompetent" or incapable of making medical decisions.

Clear and Convincing Evidence Standard[20]

"Clear and convincing evidence" is a legal standard that must be met in some states (for example, New York, Missouri, and Florida) and is required when there is no written agent or living will. Clear and convincing evidence could be repeated oral expression, as established *In the Matter of Westchester County Medical Center, on behalf of Mary O'Connor,* which states:

> The ideal situation is one in which the patient's wishes were expressed in some form of a writing, perhaps a 'living will,' while he or she was still competent. The existence of the writing suggests the seriousness of purpose and ensures that the court is not being asked to make a life-or-death decision based upon casual remarks. . . . Of course, a requirement of a written expression in every case would be unrealistic. Further, it would unfairly penalize those who lack the skill to place their feelings in writing. For that reason, we must always remain open to applications such as this, which are based upon the repeated *oral expressions* of the patient.[21] (emphasis added)

Conversations that take place should be remembered specific to time and place. For example, if you meet with a congregant who tells you what his or her wishes are, you should write down what the person said, as much word for word as possible, and make a note in your calendar as to the date that the conversation took place. (For further discussion about "clear and convincing evidence," see chapter 7.)

Substituted Judgment and Best Interests Standards

Some states allow a "substituted judgment standard," which enables someone who is close to the patient to make decisions that the patient would make were that person competent. If that is not possible, then a decision-maker should be guided by the "best interests" standard in which the person "considers the highest net benefit to the individual in question, given the available options and the person's known preferences and values."[22]

◆ ◆ ◆

As you can see, these issues are neither easy nor simple to understand, which is why it makes sense for you to know about them, since the majority of your congregants will not. Even though you are not a lawyer, and neither am I, being familiar with the history behind the Patient Self-Determination Act and the terminology that your congregant may face when dealing with a loved one who is dying can help both them and you as you work to provide guidance and support to your congregants. Knowing about how your denomination deals with these issues can also be of assistance. As we well know, knowledge is power, and nowhere else is power more necessary than when dealing with health issues and end-of-life concerns.

Chapter Three

Medical Issues

Navigating Your Way through the Hospital

Every health care institution is different. Yet there are a few ways in which they are similar. They all — hospital, long-term care facility, nursing home, rehabilitation center, hospice (and even clinics, doctor's offices, pharmacies, and health plans) — have to comply with the federal law commonly known as HIPAA (Health Information Portability and Accountability Act).[1]

This law was enacted in 1996 and institutions and individuals are still trying to figure out how to comply with it. The complexities of HIPAA have led physicians and medical centers to withhold information from those who may have a right to it.[2] Also, there are stiff penalties for violators. A review of the implementation of the HIPAA Privacy Rule by the U.S. Government Accountability Office found that health care providers were "uncertain about their [legal] privacy responsibilities and often responded with an overly guarded approach to disclosing information . . . than [was] necessary to ensure compliance with the Privacy rule."[3]

Prior to the implementation of this law, clergy could walk into most hospitals and look at the census sheet for the day to see if any of their congregants were on the list. Or, if you had a relationship with the hospital's chaplain, you could call and ask if anyone from your denomination were patients, and then the chaplain could read off the names. Today, lists are not accessible, and chaplains are prohibited from telling you if your congregant is there, unless the congregant *specifically* gives the chaplain permission to contact you. It is, therefore, most important that you inform the members of your congregation that if they or one of their family members are in the hospital, and they want you to visit them, they need to let you know. Some clergy have gotten angry with hospital chaplains for withholding information about their congregant or inconveniencing them by not giving them the information about their congregant over the phone. Chaplains are considered part of the health care team and as such are required to follow the HIPAA regulations. They can be personally fined up to $100,000 for disclosing information the patient has not specifically said can be disclosed. So no matter how much you try to cajole them, chances are they will not give you the information you seek. (As an aside, one of the proponents of this law was a gentleman who was in the hospital and did not want anyone to know. The chaplain, who knew both the patient and his pastor, let his pastor know that he was hospitalized, which was the normal practice. It was announced during the worship service that Mr. X was hospitalized and the congregation should pray for his recovery. Clearly his right to privacy was violated.)

Another way most health care institutions are alike is a policy about hours when patients can be visited. While the times may be different and some hospitals are stricter than others, clergy can often gain access to a patient when visiting hours are not in effect if it is an emergency or the patient is not doing well. When visiting hours are not in effect, you should be able to gain access by entering through the emergency department and talking with the security person there. Again, if you don't know that your congregant is in the hospital, they will not give you that information, but if you say, "Mrs. So-and-so is in ICU (for example), and I have been asked to visit her as soon as possible," most times you will be permitted in. When visiting someone in one of the intensive care units off hours, you may have to wait because of privacy issues for other patients or the comfort of the patients. Or the staff may be taking care of the patient you want to visit.

The best way to ensure easier access is to develop a relationship with the chaplains at the hospitals in your area. Most larger hospitals have a Department of Pastoral Care with either a professional chaplain (Board Certified Chaplain — BCC) or someone who has had at least some clinical pastoral education. Smaller hospitals may rely on the local clergy to assist them. If your local hospital has a Department of Pastoral Care, get to know the chaplains there. Many have processes that allow you to obtain an ID card so your entry into the hospital is easier. They may also have training opportunities in which you can participate. The time to do this is not when you have a congregant in the hospital, but rather when there is no emergency situation. Chaplains can help you navigate the hospital system more easily.

The Ethos of Intensive Care Units

When your congregant is in an intensive care unit it is because he or she needs continual observation and close monitoring. Intensive care units are sections of the hospital that utilize specialized equipment. The staff is highly trained to deal not only with the equipment but with emergency needs of patients. There are certain criteria patients must meet in order to be admitted to this highly technological and labor intensive area of the hospital. Some larger institutions have several intensive care units, for example: cardiac (CICU), medical (MICU), surgical (SICU). In smaller community hospitals, there is usually one ICU that handles all ICU patients. There are no telephones by the bedsides, nor flowers or balloons. Patients are usually not out of bed unless they are about to be transferred out of the unit because their condition does not support their being mobile. Usually patients are sedated and the nurses need to be able to provide "intensive" care to their patients; hence there are limited visiting hours.

When visiting a patient in the intensive care unit, it is of utmost importance that you ask the nurse in charge of your congregant if you can go in to see him or her. It is equally important that you ensure that your hands are washed and you wear the appropriate protective clothing. This is not only to protect you but also to protect the patient from the germs that you bring in from the "outside" world. People are not usually admitted to the hospital to "get better." They are admitted to deal with whatever is physically wrong and are discharged as quickly as possible in order that they not be exposed to viruses and germs that are not usually harmful unless one's immune system is already compromised.

It is important to be mentally prepared when you are going into an intensive care unit. There will be all sorts of unpleasant smells and sounds that may not be comfortable for you. It may feel intimidating. Be prepared for your congregant to look different. Remember, they are critically ill, so chances are that their hair will not be combed, they will not have taken a shower, their skin color will be pallid, they may not be aware of what is going on around them, they may not be oriented to time and place, and they will have all kinds of tubes and wires coming out of them that are connected to various machines.

If the patient is alert, be sure to ask him or her if it is all right for you to touch them. Otherwise, ask the nurse if it is permitted. The patient may be in physical pain and any contact may be painful. I remember visiting one woman whom I had come to know rather well from the many times that she had been in and out of the hospital as they tried to manage her cancer. One day, when I went into her room, I gently placed my hand on her shoulder. Very kindly, but firmly, she asked me to remove my hand because I was causing her additional pain just by touching her shoulder. Now I always ask if it is okay to touch someone.

Be mindful of how much time you spend with the patient. While it is not appropriate to stay only two or three minutes, your visit should not be longer than ten minutes. Be aware of how the patient is reacting (or not) and gauge your departure based on the patient's comfort, not your own.

One last thing. Do not sit on the bed, ever. Pull up a chair if you need to sit down. Needle sticks happen when one sits on the bed. Also, your germs from your clothing get on the bedding, and that might not be good for the patient. And you might make the patient feel uncomfortable or cause pain or disturb the delicate sensors that are attached to the patient's body. Hospital etiquette for other than family members is that you do not sit on the bed.

"Actively Dying"

As discussed earlier (chapter 1), our bodies are not meant to live forever, and diseases have a natural progression. For example, Congestive Heart Failure (CHF) is a condition in which the heart cannot pump enough blood to the body's other organs.[4] CHF is generally a progressive disease. There may be long periods of stability, but they are punctuated by episodic clinical problems. The natural progression of CHF would indicate that each time a person has to be hospitalized to deal with clinical problems, the body is compromised more and more, so that eventually, the heart will not be able to circulate bodily fluids effectively. Excess fluid will have to be removed more and more by external means. The heart is unable to continue to support the pumping of blood to the other organs. Eventually, these other organs of the body, which rely on the blood flow from the heart, begin to shut down and the body prepares for death. At some point, further prolongation of life only extends discomfort.

"Actively dying" is the final phase of life. It can be measured in months, weeks, days, or hours. This phrase is often used once someone's care shifts from aggressively treating the disease or illness to providing comfort or palliative care. Some patients decide to utilize hospice care, either in their home or in a facility. (Chapter 8 covers these topics extensively.)

What follows is a general description of what may be expected with an impending death.[5] There are variations on this depending on the underlying illness, other underlying problems, medications, and other factors, but these are the more common physical changes and symptoms during the last days and hours —

Slowing down of body systems

Changes in breathing patterns, which become irregular (for example, shallow breaths followed by a deep breath, periods of panting)

Difficulty breathing (dyspnea)

Congestion (noisy and moist breathing and gurgling sounds)

Decrease in appetite and thirst

Nausea and vomiting

Incontinence

Sweating

Restlessness and agitation (jerking, twitching, pulling at clothing or bed linen)

Disorientation and confusion (to time, place, who is who)

Decreased socialization — progressive detachment

Changes in skin color as circulation decreases (limbs may become cool and perhaps bluish or mottled)

Increase in sleeping

Decrease in consciousness

As death approaches, the breathing may change to what is known as agonal breathing — a pattern of slow gasping breaths followed by a period of no respiration. Sometimes there is a gurgling noise that is not usually painful for the patient, although it can be very uncomfortable for those present with the patient. The nurse can sometimes alleviate some of the gurgling by removing secretions that are in the throat. Additionally, the patient may moan, but it does not necessarily mean that the patient is in pain. The fingernail beds become bluish or cyanotic.

One should not assume that just because it appears that patients are in a coma or unconscious that they cannot hear what is going on around them. Family should be encouraged to talk to them, to let them know that they are loved and will be remembered and that it is okay for them to die. Disagreements or discussions that might distress the dying person should be taken out of the room or avoided. (For other ways to assist the family, see chapter 6.)

At the time of death, the following may occur:[6]

> Relaxing of the throat muscles or secretions in the throat may cause noisy breathing — some call this the "death rattle"
>
> Breathing ceases
>
> Muscle contractions may occur
>
> The chest may heave as if trying to breathe
>
> The heart may beat a few minutes after breathing stops
>
> Heartbeat ceases
>
> Person cannot be aroused
>
> Eyelids may be partly open with the eyes in a fixed stare
>
> Mouth may fall open as the jaw relaxes
>
> Bowel and bladder contents may be released

In addition to these physical symptoms, many chaplains who are present when a patient dies sense the soul leaving the body. It is hard to describe, but one moment the "person" is there and the next moment they look at the patient in the bed and notice that the person "isn't there" anymore. It is a body, a shell, that is in the bed; the soul, the spirit, the personality of the patient, has left.

Removal of Life Support

Life-sustaining treatment may be defined as "any medical intervention that would have little or no effect on the underlying disease, injury, or condition, but is administered to forestall the time of death or to reinstate life when death can be regarded as having occurred."[7]

When respirators and other mechanical life-sustaining devices were invented, it was with the intention that they be used as a "temporary crutch (to temporarily support the life of the patient, allowing the body to regain its natural functions.)"[8] These devices have increasingly been used to prolong bodily functions for as long as possible, "regardless of the organ systems collapsing around the one that was [now] taken over by a machine."[9]

Assuming that the proper papers and decision-makers are in place (see chapter 2 on advance directives), someone may be removed from life support. Life support usually involves: a ventilator that is breathing "for" the patient or assisting the patient in breathing; medications that are keeping the heart pumping or other symptoms from being exacerbated; or, other mechanical devices depending on the underlying diagnosis and illness.

There are those who believe that removing someone from life support is "killing them." Others argue that by using "artificial" means to keep someone alive, one is impeding the natural course of the disease and the dying process. Some family members are awaiting miracles to cure their loved one (see chapter 4). Others believe that God can do miracles with and without respirators and if the person is meant to live, he or she will do so even with the withdrawal of the mechanical device. These are very personal beliefs that are not "right" or "wrong." They are the belief system of the individual, and chances are this person is not going to be easily swayed one way or the other.

The only time that I have seen families change their minds about not removing life support is when their loved one has been unconscious for an extended period of time and it is clear, especially from the deterioration of their physical body, that the patient is beyond being able to return to the quality of life previously known. As their clergyperson, your role is to be supportive in whatever decision *they* make. Your personal beliefs do not belong in the discussion because down the road, if they took your "advice" and then regretted it, you will become the target of their anger. They need to come to the decision themselves. You can support them by reminding them what their loved one told you (if you ever had a conversation with that person about his or her wishes). You can also ask them what they think their loved one would tell them to do if he or she were able to sit up in bed at that moment and say what they would want.

If it appears that the family cannot reach a unanimous decision, an ethics consult can be requested. Most hospitals have an ethics committee that can assist the family and the medical team in determining what is in the best interests of the patient. Ethics committees do not make decisions. They make recommendations, and the patient, family, and medical team are free to either accept or reject their recommendation. Most ethics committees have been trained in mediation and can assist in this most difficult and emotionally highly charged situation.

Once the decision has been made to remove life support, you should help guide the family in saying their final good-byes (see chapter 6).

Removing the breathing tube (extubation) usually occurs without the family present, but the family can ask to be present if they so desire. Once the medical staff extubates the patient, the family can return to the room to await the ceasing of breathing and heart beat. Sometimes this happens almost immediately; sometimes it can go on for hours or days. It is hard to tell unless the respirator has been breathing for the patient 100 percent of the time. You can ask the nursing staff if they have any sense of how long it might take. But be prepared for death to occur at any time once the patient has been extubated.

If the family senses that the person is in pain, know that they may ask for additional pain medication. However, there are some side effects of pain medications about which it is important to be aware.

Pain Control

Among the general population polled by Gallup in 1997, 67 percent feared dying in pain.[10] Several years ago, the Joint Commission on the Accreditation of Healthcare Organizations (JCAHO) added pain control as a "vital sign." That means whenever blood pressure, temperature, etc., are taken, patients are to be asked about their level of pain. The patient has the right to pain relief.

An article in the *Journal of the American Medical Association* found that coming to peace with God was as important to patients as pain control.[11] Unmanaged pain interferes with a patient's ability to address spiritual concerns, deal with unfinished business, and be present with family and friends. Hospice has a good understanding of how to deal with pain, since that is their primary focus. Many doctors and nurses do not have the same familiarity with pain medications. Studies have shown that some of them have fears or concerns that are unfounded. However, no patient should be in pain and at times it falls upon the caregiver to push the medical team to provide adequate pain control. If one of your congregants is in pain, the family has the right to demand better pain control.

One of the fine lines of providing "enough" pain relief, is what is known as the principle of the "double effect." There are four conditions necessary to meet the criteria for this principle: (1) the action must not be intrinsically wrong; (2) the agent must intend only the good effect, not the bad one; (3) the bad effect must not be the means of achieving the good effect; and (4) the good effect must be "proportional" to the bad one, that is, outweigh it.[12] For example, morphine is used to manage pain and suffering. However, morphine can slow respirations. Therefore, if a patient receives additional morphine, it may hasten his or her death. Some might consider this euthanasia or mercy killing. However, it is the *intention* that makes the difference here. If the intention is to relieve pain and suffering, then more morphine is appropriate. If the intention is to hasten death, then it is *not* appropriate.

The courts have weighed in on this matter as well. In the cases of *Glucksberg* and *Vacco*, the courts determined that a person has the right to be free of unnecessary pain. The courts accepted the principle of the double effect and drew the line in terms of what is assisted suicide and what is palliative care. In these cases, the "bad effect" of death may have been foreseen, but it was not the physician's intent.[13]

Artificial Nutrition and Hydration — Yes or No?

One of the most contentious and misunderstood areas of mechanical assistance is artificial nutrition and hydration (ANH). As is the case with respirators, the ability to provide ongoing hydration and nutritional sustenance was invented to help a patient recover from surgery or trauma. It was to be used as a temporary measure until the patient's body could resume normal biological functioning. While it has given some individuals the opportunity to live productive lives (for whatever reason they cannot take nutrition by mouth, but are able to function otherwise), it has created political and religious confusion that has been carried out in the press, from the pulpit, and in the street, as displayed by the Terri Schiavo case in 2006.

Artificial nutrition is not "food." It is a chemically balanced mix of nutrients and fluids. It is "being forced into the body to keep a body functioning (not necessarily alive)."[14] Some studies show that continuing ANH creates a "bad death." The constant influx of fluids causes the body to retain the fluid because the kidneys are not functioning normally and systems in the body are shutting down. This causes additional discomfort for the patient. Most dying patients are more comfortable without eating or drinking; therefore forcing food and liquids is usually not beneficial.[15] "When a person is actively dying, the removal of ANH can actually be good palliative care."[16]

Eating is the central focus of many cultures. I recall one Italian family who just could not understand that it was more painful for their mother to eat than not. The nutrients that she was ingesting were going to feed the tumor (and enabling it to grow faster) and not sustain the rest of her body. The family thought that the removal of ANH was intentionally starving their mother to death. As bioethicist Dena Davis writes, "We need to be very careful to sort out the physiological aspects of providing nutrition from the social phenomenon of 'feeding.' "[17]

When nutrition and hydration are withdrawn (or not started), the body's metabolism changes and ketones are elevated, which produces a mild sense of euphoria.[18] This means that the fears that most people have that the patient must be in pain or uncomfortable are unfounded. Even with medical proof to the contrary, we have a psychological fear that our loved one is "starving to death," so it is important that this be addressed and openly discussed.

Brain Death

"Brain death is loss of function of the entire cerebrum and brain stem, resulting in coma, no spontaneous respiration, and loss of all brain stem reflexes. Spinal reflexes, including deep tendon, plantar flexion, and withdrawal reflexes, may remain. Recovery does not occur."[19] In short, the "brain dead" patient has died. Even when breathing and heartbeat continue, it is only because they are artificially supported by machines and medications. "Brain death" is the determination of death by neurological criteria. This may be deceiving when someone is on a respirator because that person continues to "breathe" even though the breaths are not being taken by the person — it is the mechanical ventilator that keeps the body "breathing" and drugs are keeping the heart and other organs functioning. The brain, however, has lost all function. It is very hard for families to understand brain death because of the mechanical assistance the person is receiving. Sometimes, these kinds of events happen suddenly and the family may need time to adjust: "He was just talking to me on the phone three hours ago. How can he be dead now?" Hospitals will usually work with the family to give them an opportunity to adjust, but basically the hospital is keeping a dead person "alive" and will not do so for an extended period of time. There are several tests that physicians must order to ensure that their diagnosis of brain death is accurate. These tests usually take place over a twenty-four-hour period.

When persons are brain dead, their organs may be appropriate to harvest for organ donation; hence the body may be kept in this state (with mechanical support) until the family can decide whether or not to donate their loved one's organs so that someone else may have a chance to live. Organ donation is a very personal decision. It is important that you know how you feel about organ donation before you are asked by a congregant about it. As with other decisions family members or agents need to make, they need to make the decision with your guidance. So you need to know where you stand on organ donation so that you can put your own opinion aside and help them to come to a decision that is right for them.

Terminal Sedation

For some dying patients, the profound pain that may occur when dying may not be relievable by any means other than terminal sedation. Terminal sedation uses sedatives that make the patient unconscious until death occurs from the underlying illness.[20] Some prefer to call this process "palliative sedation," since it aims at relieving pain rather than bringing about death itself.[21]

◆ ◆ ◆

In this chapter, I have tried to cover some of the medical issues that arise as one approaches the end of life. I am not a doctor, so any medical terminology used or suggested here should be checked out with one's own doctor. My knowledge has come from spending hundreds of hours in intensive care units with families, patients, and hospital staff and as co-chair of the hospital's ethics committee. What I have tried to help you understand is the importance of being present, comfortable, and somewhat knowledgeable about what happens to us as we approach the end of our lives. Spending time in an intensive care unit can be frightening for the patient and the family. The more comfortable you are in that environment, the more you will be able to be there for and with them. The more discussions you have with your congregants when they are healthy about their wishes should they become very ill, the easier it will be not only for the family but for you as well. The better informed you are about what mechanical devices can and cannot do and how comfortable you are with discussing these issues, the better and easier it will be to have these conversations with those whom you serve. It is important that you understand some of the complexities of what can happen when someone is dying so that you can be supportive and informed and know what questions to ask when the family is not able to understand or "take in" what they are hearing.

Lastly, and again, I highly recommend that you use one of the hospital's best resources for hospital care at any phase of life: the hospital's chaplain. Chaplains can be excellent resources to help you navigate the particularities of the hospital system in your area. They are also available to talk with your congregation about how to best utilize the hospital's facilities and how to have those hard-to-have conversations about end-of-life issues with their families. Chaplains are there to be of assistance to your congregants and to you. Take advantage of their expertise. It will help to strengthen your own ministry.

Part Two

Theological Issues

Chapter Four

Miracles and Cures

Those who need to be healed need to be healed, no matter their race, social standing, cultural or religious background, economic status, sex, or ailment. When people ask, "Why is God doing this to me?" or "Why did God let this happen?" they are not really interested in a discussion about theodicy. They are searching for support and comfort and healing. Healing can happen in many ways. It is important for you to be open to ways of healing other than just physical healing, which is not always possible.

I learn a great deal from every family and patient with whom I work. I receive incredible grace from them even as I seek to help them find a graceful death. They "let me in" at their most painful and difficult moments, so it is incumbent upon me to allow them to teach me how *they* cope, how *they* survive, how *they* want me to be present for them. They are the experts on how they and their family function.

Miracles with or without Respirators: Healing and Curing

I learned from family members what it means to believe in miracles. Miracles of all kinds. Miracles of death and miracles of life. One wife and mother, in response to her child's asking her what to pray for, told her daughter, "I am praying for two miracles. One is that your dad will be okay and the other is that he not suffer. He would not want to live if his mind and body were as compromised as this stroke has made him. So in praying that he not suffer, I realize that what I

49

am praying for is that if he can't return to who he was, that he die and not wake up. Both will be miracles."

Other families felt that God would provide a miracle if they prayed harder, or believed more deeply or did something "for" God. Many did not want the respirator to be removed because God was going to bring about a miracle. This perplexes me because God can do miracles with or without respirators. So if their loved one was meant to live, God did not need the respirator to bring about a miraculous cure. However, it was not my job to convince them otherwise. But I would remind them that healing was possible, even when there was not a "cure." I would begin to talk about other kinds of healing — healing of hurts, of disappointments, of misunderstandings, of fractures in relationships. As part of a graceful death, I believe God continues to provide opportunities for healing even as one is dying. So I talk with family members and patients about "healings" other than physical healing, reminding them that faith is what brought about healing in Jesus' ministry.

I also talk with them about how prayers sometimes get answered in ways that may not be the answer we want, but nonetheless they have been answered. Sometimes there is a perception that God has deserted a person or a family because a prayer was "not answered." Perhaps the prayer was answered in a way we may never understand or realize. I watched many people who thought that they had not prayed hard enough or did not believe "enough" to have their prayer answered, and therefore their loved one died because of something they did or did not do. These can be difficult situations to handle if someone else's loved one pulled through and that family said it was because God had answered their prayers. Because a family's loved one dies does not mean that God did not answer their prayer. I struggle with trying to help families come to grips with these and other questions that have no answers. I do not believe, however, that God answers some prayers because someone is a "better" person or a "better" Christian or prayed more. Defending God is not helpful to the family that feels that God has not answered their prayer. Being present with them is the best way to show you care and that God cares. Our faith is what helps us in these times when there are no answers to give.

Jesus empowered people through their faith. The faith of those that Jesus healed is often what brought about their healing. People did not stand around and wait for Jesus to come to them. The people who approached Jesus believed that Jesus could heal them. But Jesus turns it around and points out to them that their faith has made them "whole" or "well" (Matt. 8:13, 9:22, 9:29; Mark 5:34, 10:52; Luke 7:50, 8:48, 17:19).

When the woman with the issue of blood touched the hem of Jesus' garment and Jesus realized that "power had gone forth from him" (Mark 5:30), he asks who touched him. The disciples, realizing that he was surrounded by people, thought that it was a bit odd for him to ask who had touched him. Many had, but none had the need or the faith that this woman had. According to both the Gospel of Matthew and the Gospel of Mark, the woman said to herself, "If I only touch his cloak, I will be made whole." And she was made whole. Jesus, when he figures out who it was that touched him, says to her, "Take heart, your *faith* has made you well." Had the woman not wanted to be healed, would she still have been healed? I do not think so. It is in asking to be healed that we are saying to God that we want to be healed, that we are willing to be healed, that we want to be made whole, that we want to be in right relationship with God. If we do not acknowledge that there is something within us that needs healing, then I believe that God cannot heal us from it. We have to be willing to say to God, if we can, "I need your help...I need you to help me to heal" before God can work in our lives. It is in the asking to be healed that we acknowledge that we have a need to be made whole — sometimes physically, sometimes emotionally, and sometimes spiritually.

Healing does happen beyond just our physical healing. I watched as families healed rifts, resolved old hurts and wounds, and began healing from decades' old conflicts. I believe that those in the Bible who witnessed others being healed were also healed of their emotional and spiritual difficulties. I believe this is also true for family members when they are able to face the old hurts and wounds and allow the love of God to help them begin to heal.

Biblical Strength

How does my faith give me strength to deal with things that are difficult for others to deal with? How does my faith help me to serve as a chaplain, walking people into life and into death? St. Paul assists me in explaining how I am able to deal with death and life. In Romans, he writes:

> Who will separate us from the love of Christ? Will hardship, or distress, or persecution, or famine, or nakedness, or peril, or sword? ... For I am convinced that neither death, nor life, nor angels, nor rulers, nor things present, nor things to come, nor powers, nor height, nor depth, nor anything else in all creation, will be able to separate us from the love of God in Christ Jesus our Lord. (Rom. 8:35, 38–39)

In this passage, Paul displays an incredible understanding of his faith, a faith he was sharing and trying to explain to others. The letter was written after over two decades of teaching, preaching, and writing. By the time he wrote this, he had been repeatedly beaten, attacked by mobs, shipwrecked, and held in chains.

Paul's statement of faith enables me to look at death as not the worst thing that can happen to us. In this passage, Paul brings out two themes that will empower us to see that God's love can make a difference in our living and in our dying. The main theme is that God's love for us is powerful and complete. The second is that God will not desert us in life *or* in death.

The Hebrew literature does not hide death. It is seen as the "normal end of life."[1] Throughout the Hebrew Scriptures, there are notations of the deaths of important individuals.

Death was thought of as separating one not only from one's loved ones, but from God as well.[2] Paul changes that paradigm. "For Paul, to die was to 'be with Christ' and, therefore [death] could even be spoken of as 'gain' and something 'very far better' than life in this present world (Phil. 1:21–23, 2 Cor. 5:8)."[3]

Death in the New Testament is viewed in light of the resurrection of Jesus. Christ is called the first from the dead (Col. 1:18, Rev. 1:5). Death does not "separate" us from Christ (Rom. 8:38–39); death is spoken of as being "at home with the Lord" (2 Cor. 5:8); as "gain" (Phil. 1:21); as "to depart and to be with Christ" (Phil. 1:23); and as having "fallen asleep" (John 11:11).[4]

Love is the other strong theme that emerges from this section of Romans. What Paul is really talking about is God's love for us, a love that is so overarching that nothing can separate us from it. "Since God's love has done for Christians all that has been done in Christ, there is no power that can shake that love now."[5] Paul goes through a series of rhetorical questions that can lead to only one answer. Not even God will separate us from God's love. God's love, which is shown through God's Son dying for us, forms an unbreakable bond between God and the believer.[6] That is the covenant that God has with us. God upholds God's side of the covenant. It is we who do not uphold our side when we are unsure, when we are in pain, when we are afraid. Our humanity opens us up to insecurity and fear. God's love is the "ultimate security."[7] Paul believes and encourages us to believe that nothing can unsettle the foundation of God's love for us. New Testament scholar Joseph Fitzmyer, S.J., interprets Paul's belief in this way: "In all of the uncertainty of human, earthly life there is something fixed and certain, Christ's love and God's election. These are unshakable; and Christians must learn to trust them and take them for granted."[8]

Paul's questions in Romans 8:35 are questions that many of us ask when we are distressed, when we have to make decisions that are not easy to make, perhaps even when we feel a lack of God's presence. And so we too ask, Who will separate us from the love of Christ?

Paul names some of the worst situations where one might expect him to say that God's love is not present. Instead, God's love is affirmed by Paul in 8:38, when he states that nothing can separate us from the love of God — not even death. That knowledge can be transforming.

Likewise, our living and our faith are in knowing for certain that God cares for us. One way we show our love for God is by caring for God's creations. That care may find us walking someone into death and holding the family as they weep over their loss. But somehow, even as we feel the loss intensely, knowing that our loved one has died and is with God can bring us some comfort. Knowing that even death cannot separate us from the love of God brings some solace. Fitzmyer interpreted Paul's belief in God when he wrote, "Neither death and its anguish nor life and its dangers or temptations can create such a separation."[9] Faith is living in hope, even as we grieve. Faith is being open to the transforming love of God, seeing the light of God's spirit, and allowing our grief to be transformed into hope even at our darkest time. Faith is knowing that "neither death nor life, nor angels nor principalities, nor things present, nor things to come, nor powers, nor heights nor depth, nor anything else in all creation will separate us from the love of God in Christ Jesus" (Rom. 8:38–39).

The realization that in death we are actually closer to God and to Christ is clear to me because God is with us not only prior to our death and after our death, but also *while* we are dying. The experience of dying is also of God. All of our losses are a part of being loved by God. Paul, through his writing in Romans 8, is letting us know that even though we may think differently, death is not a lapse of God's love or God's presence. Knowing that God is with me and those whom I serve as they walk into death gives me the strength I need as I walk part of the way with them.

Paul spoke about his faith and God's love for us and reminded us again and again that God is the one true God. As N. Thomas Wright wrote:

This love of God calls across the dark intervals of meaning, reaches into the depths of human despair, embraces those who live in the shadow of death or the overbright light of present life, challenges the rulers of the world and shows that up as a sham, looks at the present with clear faith and at the future with sure hope, overpowers all powers that might get in the way, fills the outer dimensions of the cosmos, and declares to the world that God is God, that Jesus the Messiah is the world's true Lord, and that in him love has won the victory.[10]

This is the love that sustains Paul as he prays, preaches, travels, writes, and suffers. This is love without condemnation. This is love that justifies and glorifies. This is the love, "seen supremely in the death of the Messiah, which reaches out to the whole world with the exodus message, the freedom message, the word of joy and justice, the word of the gospel of Jesus."[11]

This is the love that I hope I demonstrate as I serve God while walking people into life and into death, and this is the love that you demonstrate when you are able to be present with your congregants as they go through their living and their dying.

Racial, Cultural, Social, and Economic Issues

Many books and journal articles have been written about the need for an awareness of and sensitivity to the nondominant culture. The importance of this aspect of caring for our congregants cannot be overlooked. There seems to be an unwritten rule that the "other" (nondominant culture) is expected to understand the dominant culture, while there is no expectation that the dominant culture needs to understand the "other" culture. In order for there to be appropriate awareness and sensitivity, it is imperative that the dominant culture work toward understanding the nondominant culture. Culture is an important part of who a patient (or family member) is, and it must be taken into consideration when discussing end-of-life issues.

As I mentioned in chapter 1, many non-Caucasians have a deep suspicion of the medical profession. This lack of trust by non-Caucasian patients and family members keeps coming up in the literature about why non-Caucasians do not complete advance directives. There are clearly several good reasons why the non-Caucasian population would be leery of doctors and, by extension, hospitals. This distrust rooted in the history of abuse of non-Caucasians by the medical profession has, among other reasons, led to disturbing disparities in health care. In "Barriers to Optimum End of Life Care for Minority Patients," the authors point out that while major efforts have been mounted to improve end-of-life care, there is "growing evidence that improvements are not being experienced by those at particularly high risk for inadequate care: minority patients."[12]

Mistrust, born of a belief that the medical profession has been (and still may be) racist (Tuskegee alone is reason enough to mistrust the medical profession), has not been mollified even after the Supreme Court ruling about separate-but-equal provisions.

In February of 1962, three African American physicians, Louis T. Wright, W. Montague Cobb, and Paul Cornely, urged several other African American doctors, dentists, and patients to file suit against Moses Cone Memorial Hospital. In the suit they asked the court to:

> order the hospital to cease denying black physicians and dentists the use of hospital facilities on grounds of race; to cease denying the admission of patients on the basis of race; to cease refusing patients the permission to be treated by their own physicians and dentists; and to declare the separate-but-equal provisions of the Hill-Burton Act and its implementing regulations unconstitutional.[13]

The three physicians knew firsthand discrimination against not only patients, but also doctors and dentists. They saw the integration of hospitals as the best way to improve health care for African Americans, knowing that a separate hospital system would never match the quality of health care facilities that were available to Caucasian patients.

The three doctors went to the National Association for the Advancement of Colored People (NAACP) local chapters and were assisted with a lawsuit through the NAACP Legal Defense and Education Fund. The case of *Simkins v. Moses H. Cone Memorial Hospital* was a landmark decision reached by the U.S. Supreme Court. In March 1964, the Supreme Court upheld a Court of Appeals ruling against the separate-but-equal provisions in the Hill-Burton program. Hospitals that were receiving Hill-Burton funds were forced to integrate. This case had a substantial effect on the 1964 Civil Rights Act, Title IV regulations, because the programs included under Title IV, such as Medicare, would have a great impact on the African American community and its march toward equality in health care.

How sad it is that here we are, more than fifty years later, still dealing with discrimination in health care. "Patients who are black or from poor neighborhoods have significantly worse processes of care and greater instability at discharge than other patients."[14] This is yet another indication of a lack of quality care for those who are not of the dominant culture of our society.

End-of-life care also has ethnic disparities. As recently as 2000, the SUPPORT Study investigators showed that in the five major medical centers involved in that study fewer resources were used in caring for seriously ill African Americans than for other patients with similar illness severity and sociodemographics.[15] This is so even though research has shown that African American patients are significantly more likely than Caucasian patients to desire aggressive life support in the event of a terminal illness.[16]

Several studies have also shown that African Americans are less likely than European Americans to have completed an advance directive or be interested in doing so. For example, one study found that African Americans were significantly more likely to feel that they would be treated differently or receive less care if they had a living will. The researchers interpreted these results as showing a lack of trust in living wills specifically and health care in general by many minority patients.[17]

The unfortunate reality of this lack of trust is that by *not* completing advance directives, the non-Caucasian community is setting the stage for exactly what they do not want to happen. They are allowing "strangers" to make decisions about their end-of-life care, since without an advance directive, in some states, decisions can be made without the input of the patients if they are not able to communicate their wishes.

Insensitivity to cultural differences in relation to attitudes toward death and end-of-life care widens the chasm between non-Caucasian patients and their caregivers. In conversations with non-Caucasian families, they would often tell me that discussing death or dying was "forbidden." They say that it is against the nature of their family to discuss such things, even if a parent is gravely ill. This is particularly true with the older Italian, Polish, Japanese, Chinese, Korean, and Hispanic families with whom I have worked.

After realizing how uneducated I was about other cultures, I decided to self-educate about what was culturally appropriate for someone who was "other" than me. I had to learn to be culturally sensitive. I also needed to accept that as part of the dominant culture, I needed to understand the "other" and not expect the "other" to adapt to or necessarily understand me as a member of the dominant, Caucasian culture. Working in a hospital, I realized that I needed to be the one to adapt and not expect "others" to adapt to my way of thinking, working, or worshiping.

While it is dangerous to speak in generalities, and, while I try to let each patient and family teach me, there are some prevalent cultural mores that can be generalized.

- Asian families usually do not want the person who is ill to know his or her prognosis. The husband or eldest son is to be told, and that person makes the determination as to whether or not the patient is going to be told and also makes the decisions about treatment.

- A survey designed to explore factors influencing patients' willingness to engage in advance-care planning found that "Caribbean Hispanic people, like Mexican American Hispanic people, appear to prefer family-centered and collective decision making."[18]

- In a study of groups of inner-city African Americans and Latinos, Latinos were more likely than the African Americans to speak of "avoiding the prolongation of dying. 'I don't want to linger. I think we are to pray for a quick death' [Latina female]."[19] Avoiding the prolongation of dying was raised in every Latino group, but was mentioned in only one African American group. African Americans "were more likely to mention access to the best medical treatments and focus on life rather than death. 'I'm not going to accept it if he [the doctor] tells me I have only two years to live...My grandmother always told me, 'Illness is the devil — you rebuke him.' I'll be the one to prove them wrong' [African American male]."[20]

- This same study found the importance of "spirituality as the primary means for patients and their families to cope with suffering and death."[21] It was a major comfort to both groups. God, religion, and spirituality were found to be "essential components of the coping process for patients and families throughout every phase of life and death."[22] One African American woman was quoted as saying, "First of all, I'd like to know that I am ready for the other side, my soul is right. That would have to be the first thing."[23]

Coping with life-threatening illness is handled differently by different people, even within the same culture. "The ways patients respond to experiences of illness result from such factors as personality, psychological makeup, family and social patterns, and environment."[24] Religious beliefs also impact the way that people handle life-threatening illnesses. All of these issues and concerns must be considered by clergy of all cultural backgrounds when dealing with their congregants and the families of their congregants.[25]

Because of these differences, I let the patient or family teach me how they deal with end-of-life issues. I hope that you will do the same.

A word about suffering, since it too is somewhat culturally specific. I believe that God does not mean for us to suffer for "no good reason." James Cone writes, "Black theology cannot accept any view of God that even indirectly places divine approval on human suffering."[26] Similarly, my theology cannot accept any view of God that either directly or indirectly places divine approval on human suffering. Jesus endured the cross for us. Jesus endured the pain for us. I do not believe that God wants us to endure physical pain for some sort of masochistic enlightenment. I do not believe that God wants us to be martyrs.

In our society, there are cultural mores that tell some that the expression of pain is not appropriate; they are used to suffering in silence. They need not suffer in silence. It is incumbent upon the leaders of congregations to provide direction in these areas. As discussed in chapter 3, no one need be in physical pain. Spiritual and emotional pain, if present, need to be discussed and not ignored, unless the patient does not want to deal with that pain. Ultimately, it is the patient's decision and your role is to be present with the patient and "be" where that person is, and not attending to your own agenda. (See chapter 6 for further discussion.)

Sexual Orientation

Whether or not we wish to honor those whose orientation is different from our own, and whether or not we "approve" of that orientation, lesbian, gay, bisexual, transgendered, and queer (LGBTQ) individuals are entitled to be treated like everyone else, including when they are ill, are going through difficult decision-making situations, or dying. They are still God's creatures and deserve to be treated with respect and dignity. For most LGBTQs, as death approaches there are many broken relationships, losses, and fractures within families that could be healed, or at least addressed by a clergyperson who is willing and open to talking and engaging the patient and family members and friends in conversations about the need for healing.

For those who have been estranged from their family, impending death can be very emotionally painful. Attempts to assist them in resolving whatever issues can be resolved, in repairing any relationships that can be repaired, in reaching out to estranged members of the family, may be helpful, if the patient has given permission.

Many LGBTQs have a family of "choice" rather than a blood-relation family. These bonds are often stronger than family bonds, since most have been through difficulties and stresses and disappointments together over the years. It is important to honor these relationships and support them, since support is not always available to these families of choice. Nonjudgment is essential in being able to be present and provide pastoral care to them. If you cannot suspend your judgment, then you should not try to assist them. Jesus commanded us to love our neighbor, no matter who that neighbor might be. If you cannot love this neighbor, then stay away.

As I wrote in chapter 1, among my reasons for being present with families whose loved one is dying is to remind them that God is nearby, that God's wisdom is at hand, that God is also grieving the loss of one of God's creations. By reaching out to those who are in pain, are scared, are dying, I am letting them know that I care for them, that I respect them and will respect their wishes. I am there as God's witness to their faith in themselves and in God. Respect and compassion are the sources from which my work with patients comes forth — just as Jesus showed respect and compassion for those who came to him for healing. The least we can do is show respect and compassion for *all* who are ill. The most we can do is be present and remind them that God, too, is present.

Chapter Five

Our Own Demons

Clergy have a responsibility to help congregants with many difficult decisions throughout life. One of the most difficult for us (as well as for our congregants[1]) is about end of life, how we want to die and what we hope to accomplish before we die.

If we don't face our own demons with regard to death and dying, we cannot empower our congregants to face those most difficult-to-face decisions. Decisions about how one wants one's life to end are individual decisions that need to be made, when possible, through a process of discernment. In addition to their religious beliefs, people have financial and familial concerns as well as the desire to be pain-free. No one can or should make decisions about end-of-life issues quickly and without prayerful discernment.

The "Prayerful Discernment Process" begins by acknowledging our fear and our humanness in being scared to look at the fact that we are mortal and will die one day. It then leads one through a discernment process as one considers the accomplishments, difficulties, and the "work" one has to do to ensure that one is prepared for the dying process (as much as one can be prepared for such a time). The process then brings God into the discussion and where one thinks or hopes God will be when one is dying. It also raises questions about our fears of dying and how we use our belief system to help allay our fears and accept impending death.

In our culture, dying is a very private experience. Just as each of us has our unique relationship to God, so we also have our own way of looking at and discerning with God how we hope dying will affect us.

Each of us values different aspects of our living, deciding what is more important to us and what is less important. Likewise, we value different aspects of our dying process. In my work as a chaplain, I have seen people who want to be lucid and find some way to tolerate any physical pain so that they can be present for as long as possible. Others want as much pain medication as possible, even if it has the double-effect of ameliorating pain but also of hastening death. Some wait until members of their family have left the room to die. Others die with family surrounding them. Some fight death to the bitter end. Some welcome death as a relief or as a welcome stranger. I believe that these are "holy" moments between the person who is dying and God.

In order to be ready for these experiences we need to have done some homework. Through using a discernment process, we, our family members, and, when possible, our primary health care providers, will know and understand what we discerned as the way we want our body to be treated as death approaches. Thinking about one's death is a humbling experience. As Christians we believe that death is another beginning. As human beings we want to live as long as possible.

Discernment is not easy, nor painless. It is compelling and requires that you be thoroughly involved in the process in order to feel comfortable not only with your mortality, but also with your decisions about your end-of-life care.

The Prayerful Discernment Process

The major focus of the Prayerful Discernment Process is a series of questions to be considered. The questions begin with contemplating what one has accomplished and what one would still like to accomplish, go through concerns and fears about dying, and ask one to consider where one sees God in one's dying. These are not easy questions and should not be taken lightly. Be prepared for some strong emotions to arise. In addition to pads of paper and pens, I usually have bottles of water and tissues handy. You will find a PowerPoint presentation of this process at *www.deathisnottheenemy.com*; some people like to read the questions and not only hear them.

(If you undertake this process by yourself, I suggest that you follow the basic outline below. I believe the process works best in a small group, so if you can bring fellow clergy together the group setting might be helpful for you and for them as you struggle with your own fears and concerns. A version of the Prayerful Discernment Process slightly adapted for congregational use can be found in Appendix 4.

Each question should be read out loud twice. Do not move on to the next question until everyone is ready. This process will take forty-five minutes to an hour or longer if you have a larger group, since sharing responses — if desired — is a part of the process.)

I suggest that some ground rules be set before beginning this process:

+ Turn off cell phones.

+ Stay present. (If you are with a group and some finish answering a question before others, all should remain "in the room" — not thinking about other things but staying focused on the process.)

+ Try not to talk during the process.

+ When you are finished, put your pen down to signal that you are done. When all are finished the group can move onto the next question.

+ If you cannot answer a question, that is okay.

+ There are no "right" or "wrong" answers, only your answers.

+ No one will see your answers. They are for you only. You do not have to share them unless you want to.

Read aloud Psalm 139:1–18, 23–24.

Opening Prayer

Holy One, we come here this day and thank You for all that You have given us and all that You have bestowed upon us. You have called us to serve You, and we do so humbly knowing that You love us just as we are and for who we are.

Holy God, we come together this day to talk about our living and our dying. This is scary for some of us so we are trusting in You to hold us as we explore our hopes, our fears, our mortality. Help us to remember that You are here with us and will never desert us.

Help us to always remember that there is nothing that we cannot accomplish when we include You in every aspect of our lives. Amen.

Reflection

* Take a few minutes to reflect on who you are and what is important to you. Think about what you have accomplished and what you still want to do. Think about the most important aspect of you (for example, your body, your mind). What is it that makes you, you?

* What do you hope that others will see as your legacy?

* What do you hope people will say about you after you have died?

* What do you think people will say about you after you have died?

* Consider how you would like to die. For example, do you see yourself in a hospital or at home or someplace else?

* Is your death sudden or is it lingering?

* Why is it important to you whether it is sudden or lingering?

* Who do you want present with you while you are dying?

* Who do you *not* want present with you while you are dying?

- Are there things you want to make sure that you say to particular people? Give some examples, if you wish.

- Do you have a bottom line in terms of what you would physically or mentally need or want to be able to do in order for your life to have meaning for you? What is that bottom line?

- What if that bottom line is reached. Do you want extraordinary measures used to keep you alive no matter what?

- Where does your belief system fit into your living and your dying?

- Where is God in your dying? Where do you see God — or maybe you don't see God?

- Do you think that God would want you to stay alive at all costs, no matter what?

- What is your greatest fear about dying?

Discuss the process: If you are doing the reflection alone, consider these questions for yourself. If you are doing it with a group, ask these questions of the group:

- How did it feel to be asked these questions?

- How did you feel as you wrote your responses to them?

- Did you learn anything about yourself that you didn't already know?

- What bothers you the most about your death?

- Are you afraid of death?

- Are you afraid of the dying process?

Here are some additional questions that can further prompt your own process and prepare you to consider how to help your congregants:

- If you have concerns, imagine how your congregants feel; they believe that you have a closer relationship with God than they have.

- How can you help your congregants to have these conversations with themselves and their loved ones?

- How can you empower them to search their souls for answers that they can live and die with?

- What do you think that God thinks of our medical technology that can prolong "life" indefinitely?

Read aloud Psalm 139:1–18, 23–24.

Closing Prayer

Holy God, this has been a difficult time for some of us. It has forced us to face our humanness in a way that is not necessarily comfortable for us. Thank you for being present with us and helping us to begin to look at these parts of our living. Remind us when we are fearful of death that You will be there with us each step of the way. Help us as we begin to have these discussions with our congregants. Let Your love and presence be felt in all those who explore their fears, their concerns, and their mortality. Help us always to remember that through our faith in You, we can live and we can die. We pray these prayers with the assurance of the love and compassion that your Son, Jesus Christ, has shown to us throughout our lives. We know that Jesus will be there to welcome our souls into God's presence. Amen.

By using the Prayerful Discernment Process, you will be able to access your own "gift of presence" as you deal with those who are grappling with end-of-life issues. Further, I believe that, having looked at your own issues regarding death and dying, you will be able to assist your congregants in a similar discernment process.

Self-Care

As clergy, we are not always willing to practice self-care. It is one of the hardest things for us to do. Unfortunately, when we don't practice self-care, our boundaries can get wobbly and our minds get easily distracted; burn-out and compassion fatigue are nearby — waiting to pounce. It is just as important to prepare for self-care as it is to prepare to preach, deal with a budget meeting, or perform other clerical duties. It is important to build self-care into your schedule and make it "sacred time," so that other things do not take over and fill up that time. Whether it is going off to read a book (not one that has to do with "work"), play golf or tennis, swim or meditate, it is time that is just as important as any other time in your day. The Gospels mention several times when Jesus went off by himself. Further, he took the disciples off for some R&R when they returned from their travels. Similarly, Jesus does not expect you to be "on" 24/7. Even God rested on the seventh day, and so should you.

When dealing with those who are dying, it is particularly important to practice self-care. While you may begin to feel more comfortable when you are with those who are dying, it is still draining and you need to be aware of your own feelings toward the person who is dying. Perhaps it is a parishioner with whom you had a long-time relationship that was meaningful to you, or one with whom you always disagreed. In both cases, it is important that you be present to that person and to his or her family and also be present to yourself and your own need to grieve.

I thought that I was very good at self-care, that God had given me the gift of being able to "handle anything" and then continue on with the rest of my day. I would "give it up to God" when I would walk out of the room or after seeing the family off the ICU or to their car. Little did I know that the residual was building up in me. Then 9/11 happened, and I spent a great deal of time at Ground Zero with the rescue and recovery workers. Again, I thought that I was doing just fine — "giving things up to God" — as I listened to stories of hurt and pain and loss and the constant questioning of "why God could let this happen."

Then I began to notice that my soul had gotten "quiet." I was not able to deal with other people's problems, nor was I interested in doing so. I didn't want to hear another story or say another prayer with someone. I was compassioned out.

This came as quite a surprise to me since I thought I was so good at self-care. I then began the process of taking better care of myself, of setting aside time for me and time for me and God. And I cut myself some slack: I allowed myself to go outside and walk around the property of the hospital when I finished being present with a family or found myself in a difficult situation that I was mediating. I took breaks. I got coffee (decaf); I talked with staff about what was playing at the local movie theater or what they were going to do over the weekend. I made sure that I put time on my calendar that was sacred time — time for just me and for me and my family.

One of the amazing outcomes of this self-care was the realization that I did not need to do it all. God would provide when I could not be there. I did not have to emulate God; I just had to do the best I could do, which included going off by myself and giving myself some down time. This was brought home to me when I took time off from the hospital to go to a conference. I returned and was immediately approached by several staff members from the emergency room who said that I should have been there and how terrible it was because Cathy's father had been brought into the emergency room with a massive heart attack and had died. They told me how sad it was and how badly they felt for Cathy, the relatively new emergency room nurse manager. I then started kicking myself for having gone to the conference. I had worked myself into quite a state when I finally saw Cathy. I went up to her and offered her my condolences and began to apologize for not being there for her. She started telling me how wonderful the staff had been to her and her family. She said that they had even come to the wake and funeral and how much that meant to her. She was a new employee, and this experience had created a bond between her and her staff. As I walked away, I started to laugh and said to God, "Well, God, I guess that taught me a lesson. I don't always need to be here. I am not that important. I should have known that You would provide — and did." I realized that had I been there, the staff would have relied on me to handle this. Instead, they took care of Cathy and, as a result, developed a much closer relationship with her.

Realizing that I did not need to do it all came as a welcome relief. Now this sounds easy. At the time, it was not. But it was what saved me from leaving the work that I loved so much and enabled me to continue to be present for those who were in need of a chaplain. But I had to be present to God to be present to others.

I will never allow myself to get to that place again. It was a dark and difficult place and one out of which it is not easy to crawl. I now do a one-week silent retreat each year, which is the greatest gift I have given to myself and to God, because this time enables me to become closer to Jesus and be refilled with the compassion and wisdom I need in order to continue to serve.

I hope that you will be honest with yourself and look at yourself and the way that you are currently working. Are you taking the time to be with yourself and with God? If not, there is no time like the present to begin to find that time.

Part Three

Pastoral Issues

Chapter Six

Preparing for the End of Life

End of Life — What to Expect, What to Do

With certainty we know that we don't know when we will die. Even doctors with their advanced technology cannot always determine when someone is going to die. As noted in chapter 3, even when life support is removed, it is not known if someone is going to die immediately. Those who are expected to die immediately sometimes live for several hours or even days while others die sooner than expected.

There are many reasons that we can suppose someone is not yet "ready" to die. Some people need to ensure that their family is going to be okay. Some people want to make sure that their spouse is going to be able to function once they have died. Some people need assurance that their lives have had meaning and that when they die they are going to be "okay"; they are not going to go to "hell" or find nothing. Those with religious beliefs may want assurances that God will be there waiting for them. While we cannot give assurances with certainty (no one has been there and returned other than Jesus), what we *can* do is help people affirm their faith and remind them of the promises God has made to us.

A "Good" Death

So what is a "good" death? There are many books and articles written about what people believe a good death means. There have been studies where people have indicated what they think a good death for them would mean. Here are the top concerns, based on these studies:

- pain and symptom management (rated number 1 on almost every study)
- clear decision making
- avoiding inappropriate prolongation of dying
- preparation for death
- relieving burdens
- strengthening relationships with loved ones
- a sense of completion
- contributing to others
- an affirmation as a whole person
- funeral arrangements made
- mentally aware
- coming to peace with God[1]

A Gallup poll in May 1997[2] found the following major spiritual concerns of Americans about death:

Concern	% positive responses
Not being forgiven by God	56%
Not being reconciled with others	56%
Dying while being cut off or removed from God or a higher power	51%
Not being forgiven by someone for a past offense	49%
Not having a blessing from a family member or clergy	39%
The nature of the experience of death	39%

With these things in mind, a good death will vary depending on the person. The best way to find out what people think is a good death is to ask them and then do what you can to help facilitate what they see as important for them to have a good death.

Family Disagreements

While we try our best to be present with those who are dying, it can sometimes be very challenging because family issues continue to be family issues — siblings continue to have the same issues they had when Mom was well. When a parent is dying, the same sibling "stuff" that was there from childhood returns. Family dynamics are magnified when family members are under the kind of stress that can be present, particularly when a matriarch or patriarch of the family is dying. The role that you can play when these dynamics are present is to act as a mediator: listen to all sides and try not to take sides. Most people just want to be heard, and once they know they have been heard, they can let the issue it go. Your role is to ensure that the person who is dying has the best possible environment in which to die and to do so in a graceful manner. Disagreements should be taken outside of the room (and earshot) of the patient. Even patients who are comatose might hear what is going on and become concerned or agitated or be aroused from resting.

If there is one family member who is in disagreement about whether to remove life support, there is probably some underlying issue between that family member and the patient that was not resolved. Another possibility might be something like this scenario: the person has been the one to take care of the dying person for the past ten years: it was the caretaker's whole life. So what will happen to the caretaker when this person dies? If you can talk privately with those who are having difficulty with removal of life support and can find out what the underlying issue is that is preventing them from letting the person die, chances are you can help them to deal with their unfinished business so that the entire family is in agreement.

I believe that family members need to be in agreement regarding the withdrawal of life support because they are going to have to continue to live with each other after the death of their loved one. Families need to be there to support each other at this extremely difficult time in their life as a family. Having one or two family members at odds over the decision will cause difficulties for the family in the future.

Let me give you an example. An elderly woman was very ill and near death. She was comatose and connected to various life support systems. Her family was with her. They were not sure whether to continue a treatment that was not working. We talked about it, and they felt that continuing to provide extraordinary measures was not what the patient had said she wanted. One granddaughter asked if there was anything else that could be done. The doctor indicated that there was one other treatment they could try but he doubted that it would work. The granddaughter pleaded that it be tried. The family agreed to give it a try. Two days later, the granddaughter called me to say that it wasn't working and she was now ready to let her grandmother die. By taking the time to hear the granddaughter's plea and trying that "one more thing" so that she could be sure in her heart that everything had been tried, this family was able to be "one" as they gathered around her bed, sitting with her until she died.

You can mediate these situations by virtue of who you are and your role in the family system. However, it is important that you not bring your own agenda into these discussions. If asked, "If this were your mother (father, spouse, significant other), what would you do?" the best response is: "She is not my relative. She is yours, and that is what matters now, not my own preferences." This family is going to have to live with its decision so it is important that they understand what they are doing and why they are doing it. The granddaughter was able to be at peace within herself and with her family and not wonder if her grandmother might have lived had they tried that one more treatment.

I learned the hard way that families show their love in all different ways. One family almost came to a physical fight over whether to remove their mother from life support. I physically had to stand between two siblings and tell them to go outside if they wanted to continue the fight. I then sat down, realized the danger I had put myself in, and said to God, "Please help me to understand what is going on here. I hate this yelling and screaming, God. Help me to help them!" What came to me was the realization that this was how they showed their love for each other. This was how they always functioned as a family, and I was not about to change it. Once I realized that, I was able to be present to this family and to handle them and minister to them. People show their love in many different ways — not necessarily the way that I would show love — but it is not up to me to judge how a family functions. This is how they have gotten through life up until now, and they are not going to change. My role is to help them through the situation in which they now find themselves. That too is your role: knowing that you cannot change them, you can only help them through the situation they are currently facing.

Forgiveness

Every faith tradition has its own way of dealing with sin and forgiveness; I am not going to go into the various ways here. Hopefully, that was covered in your seminary or denominational training. What I would like to stress here is that forgiveness for those who are dying is often of utmost importance to them, even if they are not aware of it.

In an article I wrote for the *Living Pulpit*,[3] I told the story of an eighty-five-year-old man who was dying, and was having a very difficult time with his impending death. The nursing staff asked me to talk with him because they sensed that there was something that he needed to deal with and hoped that I could find out what that was and help him. As we began to do a life review, he talked about his work as a philanthropist and how much pleasure he had found in helping those less fortunate than he. During our conversations, he seemed to want to tell me something, but always stopped short of doing so. One day I told him that I sensed that there was something he wanted to tell me. His eyes welled up. He told me that he thought he was going to go to hell because he had stolen when he was six years old. I asked him to tell me about it. He spent the next ten minutes describing in detail how he stole a candy bar from a store. I asked him why he stole it. He told me that his siblings were very, very hungry and that he hoped that the candy bar would keep them from starving. He stole the candy bar, went home, and shared it with them. He described how much they enjoyed it and how it seemed to make their world seem a little less hopeless. Then in almost a whisper he said that stealing was a sin and that he would have to pay for his sin by going to hell when he died. I then asked him to tell me about who God was for him. He described a God who was loving and open to those who sought to do good in their lives and was always there for him. I asked if he thought that God would forgive those who sought forgiveness from their heart. He said, "Absolutely." I asked him if he had sought forgiveness from God for stealing the candy bar. He hesitated and then said that he had. I asked if he thought that God had forgiven him. He paused for a few seconds and then said quietly, "Yes." I asked him if he had forgiven himself for stealing the candy bar. He started to cry almost uncontrollably. As I sat there with him, I thought about how he had carried this burden with him all his life. He was a successful businessman who generously gave to those who were most in need of food and shelter. Yet what was foremost in his mind as he lay dying was the retribution that lay ahead for him for stealing that candy bar. When his crying subsided, I asked him to pray with me. I prayed that he would feel God's love surround him, that he would be as loving and accepting of himself as God was, and that he would come to forgive himself for trying to take care of his siblings in the only way a six-year-old could manage. I also prayed that he would come to a deeper understanding of forgiveness and realize that he had spent his life trying to make up for that candy bar and had more than paid his debt.

What you might think is insignificant may have been weighing for years on the person to whom you are speaking, so it is very important that you treat that person's "sin" with as much grace as you can. Whether it is stealing a candy bar or stealing a car, when we are at the end of our life, we need to know that we are forgiven by God.

But we also need to be able to forgive ourselves for our human faults and "sins." I believe that we are much harder on ourselves than God is on us.

Life Review

Patients are the experts on who they are and the life they have lived. Telling our story is very important and telling it when we know that we are dying is especially important. Our stories are holy ground and should be handled as such. As Edwin DuBose reports on a study done through the Park Ridge Center with clergy, patients, and family members in the Chicago area, "The experiences of the dying are best understood as stories, and we show respect for the dying person by taking these stories seriously as an expression of their spiritual values, preferences, and needs."[4] Stories help us to gain self-understanding and perspective and enable us to make sense of what is going on or what went on in our past. Think about a time in your life when you have needed to tell your story and in telling it you had an "aha" moment — a moment you might not have had, had you not voiced your story. It is the same for those who are dying. By facilitating a life review, you enable the individuals to claim what they did — both the positive and the not so positive. Be careful not to judge their story or what they have done in their life. If they think that you are going to judge them, chances are they are not going to tell you the "whole" story. Try to suspend any judgment, knowing that you too might be judged on what you did in your life that someone else might find "wrong" or "inappropriate" or "bad." God is the ultimate judge of that.

You will need to build trust with those doing a life review even if they are already your congregant because they may want to talk about things that they have never told anyone and so they may need to test you first to build trust. That usually takes time, but it is well worth it. One way that trust is built is by how you respond to the person. One man started talking to me about how much he loved to garden. While I knew that his prognosis meant that he would probably not be around to garden in the approaching spring, instead of saying that to him, I asked him to tell me about what it was he liked about gardening and what he grew in his garden. After talking about his gardening for about five minutes, he said to me, "I am not sure that I will be here to garden in the spring." This enabled me to then ask him how he was feeling about that, which opened our conversation to a deeper level. It was because I was willing to go down one path with him that he then trusted me enough to take me down the more difficult path. Listening and letting him know that I was not afraid to go down that other path with him enabled him to open up to me and tell me what was really on his heart and mind.

When I do a life review, I usually start by asking what the individuals are most proud of in their life. I then ask if there are things that they wished that they had accomplished but didn't. Sometimes it is helpful to explore why they had not been able to accomplish what they wanted. I also ask how they felt when a particular event occurred or what they thought it meant. Open-ended questions are better than yes/no questions.

If I am talking with someone whose spouse is present, I will ask how long they have been married — and who chased who — which usually makes them laugh as they recall their courtship. By the way, laughter is okay. It is a part of our living — the funny stories as well as the sad stories. Tears, in moderation, for you as the listener, are okay too. As DuBose writes: "The payoff is to help the dying become more aware and more appreciative of the values and relationships that shaped — and still shape — their lives."[5]

By telling our story, we are also trying to ensure that we will be remembered, that our life has not been lived in vain, and that what we brought to this world will make a difference. You can help to facilitate that by letting them know that just by hearing their story and knowing them, they have made a difference in your life. Do listen: it is very important to those who are telling their story to know that they are being heard and affirmed. Be genuine. People can tell when you are not listening and not being genuine. Our life stories are amazing. I haven't yet heard a life story that was not filled with amazing history as well as grace. Sometimes I can see where God's hand has been particularly present in people's lives and will ask them if they were aware of that. Sometimes they have been, and sometimes they are surprised by that insight.

When children are present, and a parent is the person dying, I ask them to tell their parent about a time in their life together that they will always remember or what they learned from their parent that they will never forget. I will often ask, "Who is the most like your Mom/Dad?" And inevitably, one sibling will say, "I'm not at all like him/her." And the other siblings will respond by laughing and telling that sibling that they are definitely like their parent and go into detail with examples. Yes, there is laughter and there are tears, and both are good and necessary and healthy.

If the patient is not conscious, I will still ask the family to tell me about the person in the bed. I will ask if the family had favorite places they visited or special memories. Usually, all I have to do is ask one or two questions and the family members take over. I make sure that I listen and try (by gesturing to the patient or maybe putting my hand on the patient's shoulder) to include the patient in some way.

If you are aware of unresolved issues, you can also help facilitate those conversations. Even if the person in the bed is not conscious, these healing conversations can and should occur; I believe that God finds a way for the person to hear. One way to facilitate this is to ask the patient (when the two of you are alone) if he or she has anything in particular they want to say to anyone — if they have any unresolved issues that you can assist them with. It is important to let that patient know that whether it is anger or guilt or shame, you will help them try to deal with the person with whom they have the issue.

They may be angry at God. They may believe that God "did this" to them or has deserted them. It is important that they know that God can handle their anger and that it is okay to be angry with God. God gave us the ability to be angry. Here too grace should flow freely. Letting them know that God is present — through you — is important. By the way, you don't have to defend God. God can handle what is thrown God's way.

Another way you can be of help is to navigate the final "good-bye." If the patient is conscious, ask him or her how they would like to say their final good-byes and follow their instructions. If the patient is not conscious, here is a way that you can navigate this. First, go into the waiting room or wherever the majority of family members are and let them know that you are going to help them say their final goodbyes. Then tell them the order you are going to follow (normally, friends and other relatives first, then children and siblings, and lastly spouse, /significant other or parents). Let them know that they can spend a few minutes with the person either alone or with another member of the family (teenagers, for example, seem to want to go in with a sibling or a cousin with whom they are close). Then walk with each person into the room and escort them to the bedside. Then stand by the door. While not listening to what is being said, it is important to be aware of what is going on, because you may need to go in and give that person support or help them say good-bye or help escort them from the room. Walk them back to the rest of the group and bring the next person in. The surviving spouse or significant other or parents should be given as much time as they want or need. I do not usually stay in the room at this point, but stand outside the door and look in from time to time to see if I need to go in and be of support. I then either escort that person out, or if that person wishes, invite other members of the family back in to await the death.

If the person has already died and the family is coming in for their final good-bye, I usually ask the surviving spouse or significant other or parents if he or she wants to go in first alone, suggesting that I would then bring the other members of the family in once they were ready for others to come in. I always try to be most attentive to the spouse, significant other, or parent and let others in the family deal with those who may be having a more difficult time.

If this is happening in the emergency room, things should be handled in a similar way, except, you should go into the room where the body is and make sure that it is appropriate for the family to enter. When I first started doing this, I would make sure that the room was thoroughly cleaned up — blood wiped up, etc. Families would come in, look around, and then wonder if everything had been done because it looked too orderly. After that, I would have the staff leave a few things around and not empty the trash cans. I know that this sounds strange, but it is important that the family know that the staff did everything they could to save their loved one.

You also need to look at the body and be aware of what is present, knowing that this is how the family is going to see their loved one for the final time. If there is a tube in the person's mouth, it cannot be removed until the medical examiner has the body. Try to ensure that the sheet covering the body is clean and, if possible, a hand is on top of the sheet. Also, make sure that there are plenty of tissues and a chair or two near the stretcher. Once you have done this, go out and tell the family what they are going to see so that it will not be a total shock to them. Be prepared for anything when you escort them in. I have been surprised by some of the reactions. Sometimes there are tears, sometimes there are wails, and sometimes there is no reaction because the family is still in shock.

Use your pastoral authority to help the family deal with something they have probably never had to do before and don't know how to do. Encourage them to express their feelings to the person who is dying or has already died — both positive and negative: "Thank you," "I love you," "I forgive you." Time is the best gift you can give to them, time to be present with them, doing "nothing."

Being Present — Doing Nothing

Since I have just laid out many ways for you to help a family, it may seem to be an impossible task to "do" nothing. What I mean by "doing nothing" is not trying to make things better or fixing them.

There is nothing that you can do or say that will take away their pain and anguish. People need to go through grieving whether it is loss of limb, life as it has been, or a loved one. Being present means sitting with them in their anguish, not looking at your watch, or looking around, but focusing on that person or that family. The most surprising and grace-filled times for me were when I would sit with a family as their loved one is dying, say nothing, and have that family thank me afterward for being there. Often the comment would be: "Your presence made such a difference." This comment always came as a surprise to me since I might have been thinking that there was nothing I could do for this family or patient but be present. Their comment really reflects, I believe, their sense that my presence was a reminder to them that God was also present. I recall sitting late one night with a young wife as we sat vigil by her husband's bedside, awaiting his death. As I sat there, I started talking to God (in my head) saying how ineffective I was, how I could think of nothing to say to this young woman that was going to make a difference for her and her two small children. I kept asking God to give me the right words to say to her. A minute or two later, she turned to me and said, "I don't know how you do this. Sitting with people like me. I'm sure you have other things that you need to do, but I know why you are sitting here with me. You are reminding me that I am not alone, God is here too. And that is making such a difference for me as I try to stay here with my husband, knowing that I can't do anything to bring him back. Your presence is making such a difference for me. Thank you." God had sent me the answer. I was there to "be" and not to "do."

I think that is the best compliment I could ever receive from a family. It was at those times when I was not trying to "do" something — get more tissues, ask the nurse to tend to some need of the person dying, holding someone who was crying — it was at those times that I just sat there, as a witness, being "present." In those moments I received God's amazing grace.

In looking at how I have practiced ministry over the past twelve years, I found a thread that runs throughout the way I deal with people, both those who were dying and those who had a family member dying. That thread is a sense of God's presence, God's peace, God's love as it is manifest through me and through those I serve. My "presence" at the bedside of a dying patient sometimes enabled the patient and the family to "let go and let God."

Paul Smith's book *The Deep Calling to the Deep: Facing Death* helped me put into perspective those with whom I have journeyed as they are dying. As I read through the stories of the people that he had walked into death — people with whom he witnessed a "deep calling to the deep" — I found myself remembering patients and family members with whom I had similar experiences. My guess is that many of you have had similar experiences but were either unaware of what happened or are afraid to talk about it.

Anticipatory Grieving

When people have been ill for a long time, those around them often experience anticipatory grieving. Anticipatory grieving is exactly what its name implies — anticipating the death that is to come. This is most pronounced when someone has a prolonged illness. It can be an exhausting time for those who experience it because one is on heightened alert all the time. The next time the phone rings it could be the hospital letting them know that their loved one died. If the phone rings at an unexpected time or they hear the voice of the doctor or nurse at the other end of the line when they did not expect to hear from them, their senses go on high alert. This can go on for months or even years. It is important for you to be aware that this may be happening to those in your congregation who are taking care of someone who has a progressive illness. There are some excellent books available on anticipatory grieving and grieving in general. A list is in Appendix 6.

Letting Go

There are times when it is appropriate to give someone "permission" to die. Sometimes a person needs to know that a certain member of the family is going to be okay or be taken care of after the patient has died. This tends to come up rather naturally when a family is sitting and waiting for their loved one to die and for some reason that person is hanging on. I have been present in situations where it is clear the patient has hung on awaiting the arrival of a particular person, or the patient is waiting until everyone leaves the room before dying.

If it appears to you that the patient is unsettled about something, you can raise this with family members and see what they think. Often one member of the family will have an idea of what might be "keeping the person from dying." If someone does have an idea, it is appropriate for you to work with the family to let the patient know that, for example, the patient's child is going to be taken care of by the older siblings. Sometimes it is helpful to say, "Mom, it's okay for you to die. We are going to be okay. We will miss you, and we love you. It's okay to let go." For some reason, some people need permission to let go. I believe it is a gift family members give to that person — allowing them to die knowing that the loved ones they are leaving behind will be okay. They can "rest in peace."

What You Can Do: Cues to Help the Family

People look to clergy as the "experts" on dying, not realizing that most of us are not the experts in this area. So it is important that we model for family members what is "okay" for them to do when their loved one is dying. It is appropriate to touch the person (if it does not cause discomfort for the patient), to talk to the patient (even if the patient is comatose), to pray for the patient's death to be a peaceful one and to remind the patient and family that they are not alone; God too is at the bedside and will not desert the patient or family.

After the patient dies, it is also appropriate for you to touch the body. This signals that it is okay for the family members to touch it as well. When it seems fitting, and the family has begun to accept that their loved one has died, a prayer said, with the family surrounding the bed and touching the body, will enable them to begin their grieving process. It is important to allow some time before suggesting a prayer so that those present have an opportunity to show their emotions openly. Offering a prayer too soon forces them to stop feeling and to start "thinking." So observe what is going on and when it seems that the crescendo of tears and sobbing is subsiding, suggest that everyone come together to offer a prayer for the person who died. Your prayer, if not from your faith tradition's prayer book, might include: thanking God for the life of the person, for what they meant to so many people; reminding those present that God is also grieving the loss of one of God's creations (if that is what you believe); asking for strength for the family to get through the next several days and weeks and months; and thanking God for the love that they shared with those who now grieve the death of their loved one.

Please do not use the word "lost" or "gone": the person has died; the person is not gone, or lost. As one grieving mother, who is also a professional chaplain, wrote:

> Over and over again I have heard from parents how the use of the words "lost your child" causes them additional emotional and spiritual pain. Hearing this, I mindfully changed my language to use the more appropriate "your child died." Those are more suitable words because they speak the reality and acknowledge the enormous sense of sadness and change that continually confronts parents who contend with the challenges of life without their child. While we may think we are being sensitive in the use of words like "lost" with the hope of softening the pain or reframing the reality of death, the truth is that we are not; in fact, we may be adding to the pain.[6]

This sensitivity applies to anyone who has died. If we do not use the term "died" or "dead," those to whom we are ministering will not use it either. They will use the euphemisms that we as a society have come to use to make death seem less painful and difficult.

Rituals

For many people, rituals are very important. They are grounding opportunities: grounding one in one's faith and one's traditions. There are many books written about rituals for the end of life and I have listed some in Appendix 6. What I want to stress here is that rituals can help move people along in their dealing with what is happening to their loved one. Some chaplains include life review as one of the "rituals" they offer to patients and families. Rituals "restore a sense of order and meaning to the experiences of patients, families, staff and the clergy."[7]

It is appropriate to ask patients if they have any rituals that are especially important to them and if they wish to observe those rituals in the hospital. It is also appropriate to ask family members if they have any family rituals that they would like to observe with their loved one who is dying. It is very important, however, that you not impose a ritual on a family that does not want it. At one of the first deaths I attended to, I walked in the room, not knowing the family or the patient, acted like I was the "expert," and said, "Hi, I'm Martha, the chaplain on call. Let's gather and say a prayer for your loved one." They looked at me like I was from Mars. This was a family that did not pray — at least not together — as I later learned. The lesson I took away from that is to always ask first. I walked in like I was the expert when, in fact, that family was the expert on how they cope and how they grieve. What I should have done, and now do, is go in, introduce myself and then wait. I observe what is going on and eventually seek out one member of the family to ask about what rituals they have, if any, and ask if they think that there is anything that I can do to be of assistance at this very difficult time. Even if I know the patient's religious affiliation, I try not to assume that because they are "Catholic" that they will want a priest or because they are of a different culture or ethnicity that they will want something that I can or cannot offer them. I let them teach me what they do and how they do it. I can then facilitate either by leading them in the ritual they are familiar with or finding someone else who can. If they don't know what to do, I will ask if they have a particular belief system — like do they believe in God — before I suggest that we offer a prayer.

A word about prayer. Often we can say through prayer what cannot be said otherwise. For example, if the family doesn't know what to do about removal of life support, through prayer you can offer this as something the family needs God to guide them on. I might pray saying, "God, you know that this family is having a very hard time making the decision about their mother's treatment. There are so many possibilities and yet we know that we need to figure out what she would have wanted. Help this family to be able to focus on that and to make the decision that will be best for her. Help them also to be at peace with that decision." Or if the family is in conflict, to say that in the prayer by asking God to help them resolve the conflict so that their energy and attention can be focused on the person in the bed and not on the disagreements, and so that whatever decision is made is in the best interests of the patient.

Also, when I pray with patients, I will ask them what they want me to pray for. I have been greatly surprised and moved by some of the requests from the patients. While I would think that they would ask for prayers for themselves, instead they often ask for prayers for their loved ones or one who they are particularly concerned will not be okay after they die. I try to include in my prayer some of the words that the person has said to me about himself or herself as well as including what they have asked me to pray for. I also include a prayer for the staff — that God would be with the staff who are taking care of that patient and give the doctors and nurses the wisdom they need as they care for this person.

Lastly, a word about the staff of the hospital, and particularly staff who work in the intensive care units. These individuals have spent a lot of time caring for the patient and family. They have been with them through the ups and downs of their time in that bed. They care a great deal about those for whom they care or they would not be able to do some of the things they have to do to help someone to recover or to die. So it is not unusual to invite into the room those who have cared for the person when a prayer is being said either when the patient is still alive or when the person has died. It gives the staff an opportunity for some closure, enables the family to thank the staff, and for the staff to express their condolences to the family.

Chapter Seven

Working with Congregations

Sermons and Bible Study

Two-thirds of regular churchgoers say that the clergy at their places of worship do not speak out on end-of-life issues.[1] In a 1997 Gallup survey, only 36 percent of the respondents believed that the clergy would be "especially helpful" at the time of death, compared to 81 percent who cited family and 61 percent who cited friends.[2] Gallup described this as a "wakeup call to the clergy,"[3] suggesting that clergy needed to find better or more consistent ways to meet people's spiritual needs at the end of life. "Clergy must help people frame their lives in the larger context, so that death is understood in a larger perspective."[4]

In an opinion piece in *Commonweal*, Andrew Lustig pointed out that even though most of us know about advance directives and even the stages of dying, in conversations that he has had there is little evidence that "deeper dimensions of dying and death" are being confronted. Ironically, he notes, "faith communities — the very settings where dying should be dealt with honesty and with a sense of calm assurance — often remain places of silence, even of denial."[5]

Many of the surveys done about clergy and end-of-life issues indicate that people expect their clergyperson to be able to talk about death and dying even if they are not comfortable doing so. We are looked to as the experts in this area, and so we need to search our own hearts and souls, face our own insecurities about death and dying, and assist our adult congregants in making their own preparations for death, no matter what their age.

For example, Compassion Sabbath was created as a resource for faith leaders who want to help seriously ill and dying members of

their faith communities. It was created by the Center for Practical
Bioethics in Kansas City, Missouri. The Center invited clergy from
many different faith groups to come together to learn about end-of-
life issues. One weekend was set aside as Compassion Sabbath, during
which area clergy preached about end-of-life issues and offered various workshops for their congregants to assist them with completing
advance directives and to facilitate other conversations that need to
happen concerning end-of-life issues.

Prior to beginning this initiative, a survey was taken of more than
350 Kansas City faith leaders. The results showed that:

+ less than half of the faith leaders thought they were "very
  prepared" to minister to those who are seriously ill or dying;

+ one out of every three thought that they ministered "very
  effectively" to those who were seriously ill or dying;

+ the typical congregation's ministry did not include educational
  classes or forums on end-of-life issues, nor were there articles
  in newsletters or training courses;

+ two-thirds of the congregations did not have any programs or
  other means to teach members of their congregation to minister
  to the seriously ill or dying.

+ 82 percent of congregations did not have a program in place to
  encourage members to complete an advance directive.[6]

So when should pastors start caring for the dying? It should start
when congregants are healthy. As Ed DuBose writes,

Clergy should work to overcome the taboo of death. For
example, an occasional sermon can offer the community the
chance to reflect on death, what the tradition offers as support,
and the clergy's thoughts on the subject. Brainstorming with the
congregation through focus groups will elicit their questions and
concerns about spiritual issues and end of life. Education about

advance directives in the context of the religious community gives people the opportunity to raise spiritual issues.[7]

In a conversation with the late William Sloane Coffin about dying (he had been diagnosed with a heart ailment that took his life within a year of our meeting), we talked about how to help clergy talk about dying from the pulpit. Coffin said that he believed that clergy needed to get into the pulpit and begin by claiming their own discomfort with the topic and then work through it using their sermon.

While we may not be comfortable preaching about death and dying, perhaps that is what we need to do to break the pattern of our society. Preaching about topics such as death and dying and quality of life educates your congregation, but it also lets them know that you too are thinking about these issues and may not be comfortable talking about them. It also normalizes the topic. Hence, when issues emerge, they may be more likely to come to you for guidance.

The Terri Schiavo case has heightened the impact that clergy may have on their congregants. Since the majority of clergy who were featured in the media were against the removal of her feeding tube, I believe that there is a wrongly held assumption that most clergy and denominations are against removal of feeding tubes. This misperception may create situations where a congregant is afraid to talk with you about removal of life support for fear that you will not be supportive of its removal. This misperception needs to be corrected by you when you talk about this issue from the pulpit.

But there is another compelling reason for us to preach about and teach about end-of-life issues: it is a part of our faith and practice. We are called to empower those whom we serve, which includes giving them the resources they need to live and to die. It is part of the covenant we have with those whom we serve — the covenant to be with them in the good times as well as the bad.

Not surprisingly, several clergy with whom I have developed relationships in connection with end-of-life issues had to confront these issues when one of their congregants was hospitalized. While this is not the ideal time to have the conversation with the patient and family, it is a wonderful learning opportunity to bring back to the congregation. For example, one pastor was dealing with the two daughters of one of her congregants. The daughters were arguing about what their mom would have wanted to have done to her since her disease was progressing, and she was unable to state her wishes herself. Their conversations were escalating and getting more and more hostile. This pastor, who had tried to mediate the dispute, asked me to talk with the daughters while she sat in.

I began by asking them how they were feeling about their mother's impending death. One of the daughters started crying and talked about how her mother *was* her life. The other daughter sat there with a look of amazement because she did not realize just how much her mother meant to her sister. I asked the amazed sister to comment on her new understanding of what this all meant to her sister. This enabled them to come together and listen to each other at a very basic level. I then asked if either of them had talked with their mother about her wishes. Neither had, but the pastor recalled a conversation with their mother about a close friend when that friend was dying. This enabled a conversation to take place between the two sisters, who eventually came to a mutual decision based on the conversation the pastor had had with their mother. When the pastor and I talked about it later, she said that she did not realize the importance of that conversation with her congregant.

About a week later, she called me and said that she had not been able to forget what happened between the two sisters and that she wanted to ensure that others in her congregation did not have to go through what these two women had faced. We talked about ways that she could empower her congregants concerning end-of-life issues. Shortly after the death of their mother, she asked the two sisters if they were willing to share their experience with the congregation and asked me if I would come and discuss advance directives with the congregation. In place of a sermon one Sunday, the sisters related their experience and I talked about the importance of conversations about end-of-life issues. We then took a few minutes to answer questions. After the service, the pastor and I did a workshop with the congregation about advance directives. Forty people completed advance directives that day.

Sometimes using a situation that has occurred within your own church family is the best way to raise these issues, assuming that the ones affected by the crisis are willing to share their story. Learning through story is one of the most powerful ways to get the message across. It then becomes about "us" and not about "them."

While the Bible does not provide specific teachings and guidance relating to medical treatment of the terminally ill, especially as it relates to the use of technology to prolong life, it does provide a framework for applying biblical principles of good stewardship, compassion, understanding, caring, and knowing that even when we die, we are still in God's hands. A series of Bible study sessions could focus on different ways that stewardship, compassion, understanding, caring, and knowing relate to health issues and death and dying.

For Christians, facing the end of life may not be nearly as important as what was done with the life one lived. Since life is a gift from God, it is what we do with that gift while we are living that is of greater importance. "It is a time to live out God's will, to trust God's providential ordering and to understand life in terms of God's purpose of spiritual transformation."[8] One could use Romans 14:7–8 to preach about this: "We do not live to ourselves, and we do not die to ourselves. If we live, we live to the Lord, and if we die, we die to the Lord; so then, whether we live or whether we die, we are the Lord's."

I have not been able to find many sermons about death that are not filled with guilt in terms of being "right" with God before one dies. Several are included on my website (*www.deathisnottheenemy.com*). One of the classics is from William Sloane Coffin, who preached ten days after his son, Alex, died in a car crash. "Alex's Death" is one of the most quoted sermons about death and dying. When Dr. Coffin and I talked about that sermon, he said that his other son thought that he had "copped out" by citing too many poets. I asked if he agreed with his son's feedback. He said, "Yes, somewhat. But it was all I could do at the time. I knew I needed to get into that pulpit and talk to my congregation about my pain. This was the only way I could have done it."

Rather than reinventing the wheel, I want to share some resources that have been prepared for clergy over the past ten years. These programs are excellent, and I recommend that you take advantage of them. On the website (*www.deathisnottheenemy.com.*) you will find information to follow up on them; or you may pick and choose and create your own program based on the needs of your congregation.

Compassion Sabbath, mentioned earlier, seems to have been the most extensive program and has been replicated in many cities around the United States. On the website you will find invocations, litanies, communion prayers, suggested hymns, benedictions, rituals for impending death, and prayers by and for the dying. There is also a workbook that you can purchase from the Center for Practical Bioethics that will help you to lead a Compassion Sabbath weekend and clergy educational programs on end-of-life issues. Further, they offer *Caring Conversations,* a booklet to help people talk about what their wishes are for the end of their life. The information on how to purchase these resources is also on the website (*www.deathisnottheenemy.com*).

The Maine Council of Churches, in conjunction with other groups in Maine, came up with series of dialogues that occurred over a period of about two years. Experts were brought in to talk about some of the topics. Your local hospice, hospital, funeral home, or organ donation network would be glad to have someone talk with your congregation about these issues. The chaplain at your local hospital can also be of help in many of these areas. In Appendix 5 and on the website you will find information on the following programs:

EndLink: An Internet-based end-of-life care education program created twelve activities to encourage participation of faith communities in end-of-life care.[9]

The Florida End-of-Life Education Enhancement Project was a model program developed in 2003 to provide clergy education on loss, dying, and death. A product of the project was the creation of consumer-oriented educational materials that clergy can give to families.

The University of Hawaii Agency for Health Care Policy and Research and University of Hawaii Center on Aging spearheaded a discourse on caregiving and end-of-life choices in religious communities. They developed a handbook to "provide references and general outlines for churches and temples to follow in promoting education and stimulating discussion on issues of caregiving and end of life."[10]

Having "Those" Conversations

"For many families, the process of preparing advance directives can raise important issues of values, faith and spirituality. For that reason, people often involve clergy."[11]

In chapter 2, I wrote about advance directives from a legal standpoint. Here I want to consider them in a religious context. Joseph Fins, M.D., has proposed an understanding of advance care planning that I think is compelling and speaks to us as clergy. He believes that when one appoints a health care agent, one is establishing a covenant between two people.[12] That notion has stayed with me and is basically how I have helped people make those most difficult decisions for someone else. Dr. Fins took his definition of "covenant" from the *Baker Encyclopedia of the Bible,* which reads in part:

> The essence of covenant is to be found in a particular kind of relationship between persons. Mutual obligations characterize that kind of relationship. Thus a covenant relationship is not merely a mutual acquaintance but a commitment to responsibility and action. A key word in Scripture to describe that commitment is "faithfulness," acted out in a context of abiding friendship.[13]

Fins makes the argument that the relationship between a patient and their agent goes beyond words and beyond written documents. It is based on the covenantal relationship between the two people, a relationship that is based on faithfulness and love and that has a greater depth to it than a contract. Contracts are based on mistrust; a covenant is "based on trust and is about fidelity, wisdom and love."[14]

So when does advance care planning start, if one takes it on as a covenant? I believe it begins when a person decides to join a particular church and makes a covenant with that church and, thereby, with its pastor.

As the pastor, among your duties under that covenant is to ensure that your congregant is informed about all the different ways that the congregation can be of help. One of these duties is to ensure that your congregants know what may be in store for them when they are ill. In addition to the expectation that the person will be visited either by you or by another person in the community, you now have knowledge that can be passed onto your congregants. Namely, you now understand some of the issues that arise when someone is ill and/or dying. Under this covenant, it is your obligation to let your congregants know about these issues and help them navigate them. The best time to do this is when people are healthy, not when they are being rolled into the emergency room.

As I mentioned earlier, preaching about dying is not easy, and chances are that your congregants are going to be uncomfortable with it, at least initially. But if you frame your sermon (or Bible study) on this notion of covenant, with the understanding that covenant includes providing them with information that can be helpful to them, I believe that your congregants will be more open to your talking about death and dying. But you also need to get over your own discomfort. Maybe that is what your sermon could be about: your own discomfort and how you are working to overcome it, as Dr. Coffin suggested.

There is another aspect to consider: knowledge is power. For those who do not understand the implications of not appointing someone to be their health care agent or surrogate, it is our obligation to help them to understand. Why should only those who have the financial means to hire a lawyer have these protections? This is a justice issue. Without knowing what can happen if they don't appoint someone to make their health care decisions when they are unable to make them for themselves, people can't make informed decisions and therefore are at the mercy of health systems.

The Clear and Convincing Evidence Conversation

One of the ways that you can provide assistance to your congregants is to be able to provide clear and convincing evidence should the need arise. Whether it is to convey to an ethics committee what your conversation was or help a family member who is appointed the agent to make a difficult decision, having had that conversation will be of benefit. "The reality is we're all going to die, and to acknowledge that means we can move forward and make it more humane and compassionate."[15]

In order to provide clear and convincing evidence, you will need to know specifics as to time and place and, when possible, be able to quote the person. My suggestion is that when you have a conversation about someone's wishes concerning end of life, you make a note in your date book or in a file that you can easily access. Write down where you met, when you met, and as much of their exact wording as possible, using quotation marks to indicate what they actually said and placing it in as much context as possible. For example:

Jane Doe and I met this morning at the ABC Coffee Shop for breakfast. During breakfast Jane mentioned that she was concerned because she did not have any relatives who lived close by and worried about her health issues, since they were getting worse. I asked her if she had appointed someone as her health care agent and she said no, although she said, "I intend to make my nephew John my agent." I then asked if she knew what she wanted if she were in a condition where she would clearly not be able to recover. She said, "I want everything tried, but if it doesn't work, I don't want to be hooked up to any machinery that is going to keep me alive." I then asked her if that included nutrition and hydration, and she said, "Yes, it does." I assured her that I would make a note of our conversation and assist her nephew if there came a time when he had to make that decision. Jane expressed her gratitude for my willingness to be there for her and her nephew.

Having these kinds of conversations is helpful to your congregants and to you. It brings you closer to your congregants and it helps them to know that you are going to continue to watch over them, even as they are dying.

Another consideration is the amount of time you will need to spend on issues like this when they arise. If you have had conversations with your congregants and know their wishes, it will be a much shorter conversation with health care providers and family members than if you did not have the conversation. Remember the clergyperson dealing with the two daughters. Had she realized how important her conversation with their mother had been, she could have helped them in a more timely and less emotion-filled way and enabled them to spend whatever time they had left with their mother with her, instead of arguing about what their mother might have wanted.

The Nuts and Bolts of Advance Directives

Those who have recently faced a situation in which their loved one approached the end of life are much more likely to have thought about their own end-of-life treatment and planned accordingly.[16] Therefore, a good place to start is with those congregants who you know have dealt with end-of-life issues with a loved one. One way to involve them is to meet with them and let them know that you want to work with the congregation on end-of-life issues so that, unlike the situation with their loved one, others will be more prepared — and that you would like their help. They may be willing to talk about their experience to the congregation or write about it for your congregational newsletter. Unfortunately, what compels people to start talking about advance directives and what they want and don't want is hearing about someone else's difficult situation. More people talked about their wishes during the Terri Schiavo fiasco than had previously, and, because of that situation, more people completed advance directives.

In addition to asking your congregants to tell their stories, you can ask the chaplain from the local hospital to come and talk about situations he or she has had to deal with. The chaplain will make a compelling case for people to complete advance directives, because it makes everyone's job easier when the conversations happen when people are healthy enough to convey their wishes.

In one program, for example, I preached a sermon called "A Chaplain's Prayer" (which you will find in Appendix 7) and then, following the service, led the congregation in a workshop during which they completed their advance directives. We made copies for them to provide to their designated agent, their doctor, their local hospital, and their own records. The church also kept a copy in the pastor's office.

If you decide to do a workshop with your congregants, you can use the Prayerful Discernment Process adapted from chapter 5 (see Appendix 4), or you can use one of the many tools available to assist people in having these conversations with family or friends. You will find these resources in Appendix 3 as well.

If you choose to use the Prayerful Discernment Process, you can adapt the questions at the end to apply to your workshop, as indicated in Appendix 4. Additionally, here are some prompting questions for you to consider as you plan your time with your group:

+ How can I help my congregants to have these conversations with themselves and their loved ones?

+ How can I empower them to search their souls for answers that they can live and die with?

By using this discernment process, individuals, their family members, and, when possible, primary health care providers, will know what the individuals have discerned as the way they want their body to be treated as death approaches. And you as their clergyperson will also know so that you can assist them with decisions and can be present with them through their dying process.

Not only will the discernment process be helpful for your congregant, but it will also be helpful for family members, who sometimes have to make decisions that they would rather not make. Imagine the pain for a family, having never had a discussion with their mother about her wishes for end-of-life care, when they are placed in a situation where cardio-pulmonary resuscitation (CPR) is needed to save her. What if the quality of her life is not going to be what the family believes she would want, but they have never talked about it with her? What decision do they make? Will it be the correct decision? Will it be "what Mom would have wanted?" Without Mom having gone through a discernment process, which she then shared with her family, there is really no way to know. And yet families face painful decisions like this every day. The uncertainty of making the "right" decision can be greatly influenced by conversations that occurred when the patient was able to express what she would want in the event her health failed.

You can also empower your congregants to have conversations about end-of-life issues with their family members. Encourage them to do the following: Invite everyone over, sit around the kitchen table with coffee and something to eat and start talking. The conversation should be about how they want their body treated in the event that they are unable to communicate their wishes. Initially, if it is a parent starting this conversation, one of the children will say, "Oh Mom and Dad, you are going to live a long time. We don't need to discuss this now." (I said this to my own parents!) It is uncomfortable for children to think about their parent dying, but the parent needs to insist. There should be lots of tissues because there will be tears, and there will be laughter and there may be some strained moments, especially if the child does not agree with what the parent does or does not want done. If the parent wants to choose one of their children as their agent, they need to make sure that the child agrees to follow their wishes. The reason I suggest that the entire family be together when these conversations take place is that down the road, this will help when that one sibling has to make the decision and can say that they all heard their parents' wishes and those wishes are being followed. It makes for less sibling friction when everyone hears it at the same time from their parent.

Everyone at that table who is over the age of eighteen should complete a proxy form. As we know, death comes to all ages, not just those who are the elders of our congregations.

And make sure that you and your family have had the kitchen table conversation as well so that you can say, "I have done mine too."

Chapter Eight

Knowing the Options

Jesus bid us to visit the sick (Matt. 25:36) to remind people that they are not alone, that they are a part of a community. God did not desert Miriam after she spoke against her brother Moses and was stricken with "white scales," making her "unclean" (Num. 12:15). During the seven days that Miriam was "shamed," her community did not leave her, nor did God.

Jesus demonstrated through his ministry the importance of community when we are most in need. We tend not to notice the miracles that occurred in the community when people reached out to help each other. For example, in Mark 2:3–5, when there were too many people crowded into Jesus' home, some men lowered a paralytic on his mat through the roof so that Jesus might heal him. "When Jesus saw their faith, he said to the paralytic, 'Son, your sins are forgiven.' "

Our society encourages people to be individuals and to put "me" first. The power of community has been lost. My work as a chaplain enabled me to remind people that they are not alone and that they are part of a community. It also allowed me to remind them that they are part of a faith community and are not alone in their suffering. God is there with them along with their faith community.

Even strangers can be a community when the need arises. This was demonstrated to me one morning when I was spending time with a family in the critical care unit. This family, a husband and wife, were keeping watch over their daughter, who was very ill. In the waiting room, they had met two young women who were awaiting word of the outcome of their mother's health struggles. They also met a wife and son who were watching over their loved one, who had not done well following major surgery. These three families, meeting in another place and time, might never have found their way to becoming as supportive and loving as they were to each other. But because of the circumstances they were in, they all found it easier to cope. Why? Because they gave each other the support, the love, and the comfort they needed. They cried on each other's shoulders, they laughed together, they cheered good news, and cried over bad news. These six people showed the power of strength in community, even a thrown-together community. These strangers demonstrated how we can help each other when we come together as a community, particularly in times of crisis and change.

Congregational support is important, because you as the clergy-person should not be ministering alone. The community should be sharing in the visitation, praying, and being present with those who are ill or dying. "God suffers with each of us in our own personal suffering. God also loves and cares for each of us and calls us to be examples of that love and care to each other. Pastoral care of the terminally ill is an explicit response to God's command to 'love your neighbor as yourself.' "[1]

Isolation when one is dying can be profound. As a society, we shun those who are dying, remove ourselves from them, and leave them to die without people around, other than the immediate family (sometimes). Community is at the heart of our religious beliefs. We worship together each week and come together for celebrations and for rituals. It is important that those who are dying know that they are not forgotten. While they are entitled to their privacy, it is important for the religious community to provide support in whatever ways might be acceptable to the one who is dying and to his or her family.

Even though it may be scary for them, encourage your congregants to reach out to those who are ill and those who are dying and to their families. Suggest to your congregants that rather than saying, "What can I do to help?" to say instead, "I am going to the grocery store today. What can I get for you?" This kind of offer is easier to hear and respond to. Ensuring that family members get a break by offering to stay with their loved one can be quite helpful. They need a break, and offering to drive them somewhere or run errands for them is most appreciated. But it is also important not to just "do" for them, but to be present with them. Suggest to your congregants that they sit and have a cup of coffee with the sick person — just be present, not to have the answers, but to be a listener. They can hold the hand of the person who is dying. Read psalms or a newspaper if that is what the sick persons want. The visitors don't have to make small talk. Instead, they should try to be present with the person and talk when they want to talk and not talk when they don't want to talk. The most important thing for pastoral visitors to remember is that they are there to remind the family that they are not alone in their time of distress or grief or illness. God is there too.

There are many books and other resources available to train lay pastoral visitors. You can adapt the material from Compassion Sabbath, and the Maine, Hawaii, and Florida educational projects. I highly recommend that you have your congregants read and discuss *Tuesdays with Morrie*. This is an excellent resource in terms of hearing from someone who is dying and also seeing how Mitch Albom, the author, dealt with being there for Morrie and the things that he did that were helpful and were not helpful.

Mike Graves, Ph.D., wrote a section in Compassion Sabbath called "Proclamation Resources for Caring for the Dying."[2] It is an in-depth look at how to help your congregation to actively minister to those who are dying. You will also find this included on the website (*www.deathisnottheenemy.com*).

Hospice

Only 24.9 percent of Americans die at home even though more than 70 percent say that is their wish.[3] Approximately 2.5 million people die in the United Sates each year. Approximately 80 percent have a protracted illness before death and yet less that 20 percent use hospice or palliative care.[4] In the last years of life, health care costs are more profound. "One recent study found that, for those alive at age eighty-five, one-third of life-time health costs are still ahead."[5] According to a report from the Medicare Payment Advisory Commission (MedPAC), about a quarter of the total Medicare budget is spent on services for beneficiaries in their last year of life, 40 percent of it on the last thirty days. In 1997 Medicare paid an average of about $26,000 per person in the last year of life, or six times the cost for survivors.[6] There are ways that clergy can assist their congregants in making informed decisions about how to live out those last years, months, weeks, and days of their life in ways that are meaningful and important to them. Knowing the options is one way that clergy can empower their congregants so that those who wish to die at home can do so, and those who do not, do not have to spend whatever money they have saved in order to cover the costs of their health care as they approach the end of life. So encourage your congregants to get the best assistance possible when they move from aggressive care to comfort care.

Unlike a hospital, hospice provides support for the entire family and deals with the social, emotional, and spiritual issues that may arise. Hospice provides patient-centered palliative care for the terminally ill, combining emotional, spiritual, and social support with expert medical and nursing care delivered by an interdisciplinary team of specially trained health professionals and volunteers.

Hospice care is usually provided at home. Families adjust their work and life schedules to provide the majority of the care to their loved one. Homes are transformed into caring places with hospital beds and other equipment that might be needed to keep the patient comfortable. Family members are trained to administer medications and can bathe and turn the patient as needed. The nurse, aide, social worker, chaplain, and hospice volunteers stop by on a regular basis and assist as needed. If the family is not able to provide the care needed in order for someone to stay at home, there are some hospices that have their own residences or contract with hospitals or long-term care facilities to "utilize their beds" for hospice care. If a family is unable to take care of their loved one at home, chances are they are going to feel guilty about that. Rather than say "Don't feel guilty," try to talk it out with them and help them to come to a new understanding of how they can be present with their loved one even if the setting is not at home.

Someone who is on hospice has an "out of hospital" do-not-resuscitate order, so when their heart stops or they stop breathing, 911 is not called. If 911 is called, it is presumed that the patient or family has changed their mind. The emergency medical technicians do whatever they can to resuscitate the patient and will transfer him or her to the emergency room.

Hospice has been underutilized by doctors and by families. Some people assume that their doctor will offer hospice. That is not always the case. Being an advocate in these situations is important for the patient and the family. Waiting until two or three days before death is almost too late for hospice. Once a terminal diagnosis is made (and it appears that the person has about six months or less to live), a person can be placed on hospice. This decision can be reversed at any time and the person can then resume aggressive treatment. While on hospice the patient will continue to receive medications and can receive treatments for palliation; these are not curative but do provide comfort, for example, radiation to shrink a tumor that is causing pain. The patient lives as normal a life as possible, depending on the severity of the illness. The phrase "there is nothing else we can do" is not in the vocabulary of hospice staff. There is always something more that can be done to ease a patient's anxiety, pain, or discomfort.

Palliative Care

Palliative care is "an approach that improves the quality of life of patients and their families facing the problems associated with life-threatening illness, through the prevention and relief of suffering by means of early identification and impeccable assessment and treatment of pain and other problems, physical, psychosocial and spiritual."[7] All hospice care is palliative care. All palliative care is not hospice care. "The goal of palliative care is to achieve the best possible quality of life through relief of suffering, control of symptoms and restoration of functional capacity while remaining sensitive to personal, cultural and religious values, beliefs and practices."[8] Palliative care should be an applicable approach throughout a person's treatment, not just at the end of life.

Palliative care can be provided in a hospital or an out-patient setting or in a long-term care setting. It works to reduce the severity of symptoms and is appropriate at any time in the course of an illness. It can be provided while one is receiving aggressive treatments — unlike hospice, where aggressive treatment is not pursued. It provides symptom management. There is usually a treatment team, similar to hospice, which includes doctors, nurses, social workers, and chaplains who specialize in palliative care. This team works with the patient and family on medical decisions and goals of care. Many hospitals are now including palliative care teams as an option for patients.

Long-Term Care and
Assisted Living Facilities

We are living longer, with pneumonia no longer considered the "old man's friend," since we have antibiotics to treat it. Joanne Lynn[9] has said that the average American male is now debilitated for five years before he dies; the average American female for eight years before she dies. The major causes of death are all progressive, degenerative illnesses that leave people in fragile health for a long period of time before death.[10] Therefore, we need to be prepared for people living longer and needing more "hands-on" care than was previously needed. Long-term care is one of the areas that will be most impacted by our living longer.

Long-term care is "a variety of services that includes medical and non-medical care to people who have a chronic illness or disability."[11] It can be provided at home, in the community, in assisted living facilities or in nursing homes. It meets health or personal needs and is designed "to assist people with support services such as activities of daily living like dressing, bathing, and using the bathroom."[12]

In 2009, about 9 million men and women over the age of sixty-five needed long-term care. By 2020, 12 million older Americans will need long-term care. Most will be cared for at home; family and friends are the sole caregivers for 70 percent of the elderly. A study by the U.S. Department of Health and Human Services says that people who reach age sixty-five will likely have a 40 percent chance of entering a nursing home. About 10 percent of the people who enter a nursing home will stay there five years or more.[13]

Some long-term care facilities are what used to be called nursing homes. They are now known as long-term care or rehabilitation facilities.

There are also continuing care retirement communities (CCRC), which have what are considered step-down services. Where you live depends on what your needs are. For example, when you first move in, you may be in an apartment, taking care of your own needs, cooking your own meals, driving your own car, etc. Then as your health declines, you may begin to have someone come in to assist you from time to time ("assisted living"). Eventually, you may need to move to a different part of the facility where you can be taken care of in a more controlled environment and eventually be moved to a "skilled nursing facility," where your needs for care are more involved. CCRCs usually charge an entrance fee to move in and ongoing monthly fees as well.

If you are working with a family on arrangements for any of the above facilities, be sure to encourage them to ask questions about the levels of care and the level of nursing care provided. Also, encourage them to talk with their health insurance carrier as well as any other insurance carrier they have to ensure that the costs are covered.

Lastly, it is important for your congregants that you maintain the ties that bind these parishioners to their congregation. Visits from pastoral visitors as well as from their clergyperson remain an important touchstone. Many people's greatest fear is being forgotten. You can allay that fear when you ensure that they are visited by members of the congregation and by you.

Chapter Nine

Focusing on Transformation

This chapter was the hardest to write. I wrestled with defining "transformation," which I felt I needed to do in order to be clear about what I mean by transformation. People have been trying to define transformation for centuries and there are as many definitions out there as there are people. I can write easily about what transformation has been like for me and what I have observed in others, but to define it is not so easy. So I asked several of my chaplain colleagues to define transformation for me. Below are some of their comments:

The Rev. Stephen Harding

Over the six years that I worked as a hospice chaplain, I worked with a lot of people who died. Being involved with death several times a week helped me come to terms with my own death and my patients and their families taught me a great deal — about living and about life. After about four years of hospice work, I started to ask why am I doing this work (that is, why am I here?). Gradually I began to realize that what I was witnessing was the transformation of my patients from this life to whatever is next, that I was privileged to help them on a part of their journey to whatever is on the other side of death. Underneath this realization is the Christian belief that "life is changed, not ended" because of death — that we continue on in some way. I believe that when we die, we return to God. Of what happens after that, I am less sure.

After a while I realized that I too was changing because I was involved in my patients' transformation from this life to the next and watched as they were transformed by death. In some way, seeing their external transformation from life to death gave me the strength and confidence to be able to make my own internal transformation into much more of who I am. I was able to become more complete in myself than I had been before.

I think that the transformation of an individual may come about because of some large event or a series of smaller events that shake up or challenge one's perceptions of oneself and one's relationship with oneself and with the world. ("Traumatic events call into question basic human relationships. They breach the attachments of family, friendship, love, and community. They shatter the construction of the self that is formed and sustained in relation to others. They undermine the belief systems that give meaning to human experience. They violate the victim's faith in a natural or divine order and cast the victim into a state of existential crisis" [Judy Herman, *Trauma and Recovery,* Basic Books, 1992, 51, in "The Hospitable Hermitage: Where the Hearts of God, Self, World and Others Meet," by Richard Fournier, downloaded from *www.thomasmertonsociety.org/rich.htm*, February 23, 2009]).

In terms of a community's transformation, I would posit that the large event or the series of smaller events would have to challenge the underlying assumptions of that community, e.g., the town in New Jersey where high school athletes raped a learning disabled girl; the hazing of younger players on a spring training baseball trip of a team on Long Island.

In thinking about these two, and then about Katrina, perhaps the sentinel event or series cannot be overwhelmingly devastating, like Katrina. But perhaps the outside event needs to serve as a catalyst for an awakening as to what is truly important — the "false self" is no longer an option. Or, maybe it's something as simple as the behavior of a member of a congregation toward an outsider or the death of a young parishioner that galvanizes everyone else to rethink their approach and who they are.[1]

Chaplain Jane Mather

When we come face to face or heart to heart with some very familiar or brand new aspect of God and allow ourselves to pay attention to it — take it in, so to speak — we are transformed. Jacob wrestled with the angel; Saul became Paul when out and about. But in their dreams and daily walk, they encountered God face to face and were forever different! I guess a bad dream and being struck blind could be considered like being diagnosed with cancer, but what about the burning bush? Moses "stepped aside to see" and I believe that if we "turned" to see more often we would be daily transformed in small and wonderful ways. Perhaps transformation comes in whatever form we're willing to allow it. Some need a kick in the rear; others may only need a sunset.

I guess besides the means, it might be good to think about what we're being changed "from" and "to" in transformation. Having worked from a religious perspective with the dying for so long, I believe that transformation is a gradual awareness of our immortal nature while still living as mortals. To the degree that we can accomplish that with our senses — take in the sunsets and the vulnerability and beauty of new life — the process begins. But we see through the glass poorly and the image of the divine is so counterintuitive to the senses with which we're equipped. The fullness of our immortal nature seems to take the death process to achieve fully: shedding mortality and its scripts and costumes doesn't happen here! But I think we pray, worship, discipline ourselves, and hunger for it along the way, and to the extent that we yield to the encounters with the Divine enroute, I think we live full, rich human lives in some measure of awareness that there's more than the dross of the scripts and the costumes. Then the final letting go is perhaps less painful. But even Jesus said, "if possible, no thanks...nevertheless, I totally trust You, God." Our human experience seems to need some fire, some crucifixion, and some duress. I just think the less we take to the deathbed of fear, clinging, and bitterness the more we come through without feeling like we've been burned![2]

The Rev. Sarah Fogg, Ph.D.

I think "transformation" is equal to or means "changing shape." It can be changing of a physical shape (one's body, for example), or of less physical or tangible things, like one's thinking, perspective, worldview, behavior. It usually happens as a result of something breaking — a breakdown/up (in body, structure, relationship, previous worldview or understanding, etc.) or a breakthrough/out (something is seen or understood differently by no longer seeing or understanding something in the previous way).

These breaks can be either positive or negative in their consequences. I think chaplains minister to people who are going through some sort of breakdown or breakup that is usually having negative consequences for them. Our mission is generally to assist them in achieving a breakthrough or a breakout that has positive consequences. Physicians have a parallel function; their focus is usually physical. The counseling focus is usually emotional or mental. Ours is usually of a spiritual nature.

Once in a while, a breakdown can be immediately restored to what it was (snapping a dislocated bone back into place, finding a lost child), but most of the time, "new glue" is needed even to put something back just as it was. For those things that can or should never go back to their former shape, it takes a while to fiddle with the old parts, discarding the no-longer-useable and locating new ones before the new shape can fully have life that works. That seems to always need a community, some kind of "other" for assistance. (Adam was given Eve, God called his people together, etc.)[3]

The Rev. Jill Bowden

The image of "transformation" is, in my mind, a Monarch butterfly chrysalis. It is a pale green architectural marvel formed by a "brainless" worm that preserves its life through months of disastrous climactic changes and is discarded without a thought at the moment the miraculous butterfly emerges, capable of flying thousands of miles on wings that can be destroyed by a curious finger.

Transformation happens in every conscious moment and is gone — like enlightenment — the second we recognize its presence. When the thinker owns the thought, when the transformed recognizes its transformation, the miracle is once again beyond reach. But it is never over; it always comes again, and again, and marvelously again, until the emotion wells up and we stand in baffled humility at the immensity of the gift — and dimly begin to sense the Giver. And then, it is gone again.

Transformation happens even when we are unconscious, when we are living "the unexamined life." But once our eyes are opened, there is no turning back. We cannot un-know what we know, we cannot turn it off again. "The examined life" is strenuous, but it has deep rewards in awareness of the transformative process in each moment of living. To embrace it intellectually is exhausting; to let it embrace you is like coming home to a place you have only dreamed, and finding your deepest reality there.[4]

◆ ◆ ◆

These definitions by my colleagues are so individual and yet encompass so much of what I too believe transformation can be. I continued to wrestle, much like Jacob did with the angel, with how to best define transformation. Then, at an Ash Wednesday service, the homilist talked about metanoia (μετάνοια). The literal meaning is "changing one's mind," which is the way it is used in classical Greek.[5] In the Bible the translation involves remorse for one's actions and is necessary to rebuild a relationship with God. It involves a public confession of sinfulness and a genuine desire to change. Another definition would be "to turn away from" with the realization that what one turns from is wrong and what one turns toward is correct. In the Septuagint the emphasis is on turning back to God. In this homily, however, the homilist gave it a slightly different meaning. He defined *metanoia* as "to turn another way or a new way." He was talking about it in the sense that Jesus came to encourage people to turn another way — away *from* the Law and *to* God. So, as I sat there listening to him some dots started connecting — by changing one's mind and one's actions (for example, by turning another way or a new way,) might one be more open to being transformed? Therefore, for my purposes, transformation is when one turns another way or a new way as Jesus did when he showed by his words and his actions that he stood with the disenfranchised, the poor, and the outcasts.

Like my colleague Rev. Stephen Harding, whom I quoted earlier, over the eleven years that I sat with people as they were dying, I was transformed by death. I came to understand that death and dying were "holy moments." I came to feel a profound sense of peace in facing death and dying as I realized that God was present; God had not forsaken the person in the bed. God was quietly, awesomely, present at the deathbed. Out of these experiences, my theology became much more connected with those whom I served as they were dying. My sense of God and God's love was transforming as I walked people into death. At some point, as I sat with someone who was dying, I realized that I was not afraid of death. Having sat with those who were dying, I realized that God was present and therefore there was nothing about which to be afraid. I turned a new way through being with those who were dying. That was a transforming moment for me. The holiness of that moment is transforming. I am not trying to romanticize death, but rather put it into the perspective of our living and our dying as both being a part of the realization that we are fully human.

So what does one do to transform people to help them turn another way? I thought that I could "do" something and people would somehow be transformed. But I came to realize that transformation is a process. It is not just thinking differently or acting differently. Transformation is an act of trust. It means coming to a new understanding in your "core," in your "soul," as you turn to a new way of seeing and thinking.

Transformation for Those Who Are Dying

In Romans 12:2, Paul writes: "Do not be conformed to this world, but be transformed by the renewing of your minds, so that you may discern what is the will of God — what is good and acceptable and perfect." I am not going to claim that having a life-threatening illness transforms people. There are plenty of books and articles that cover that sort of "cancer is the best thing that ever happened to me" scenario, and I do not deny that a life-threatening illness can transform someone. Instead, I want to talk about transformation that comes from our faith, a faith that enables us to turn to something new, to see differently. "In the transformation of faith we do not become more of what we are but of something 'different' or 'new.' "[6]

Christianity is transforming. One cannot be a Christian and not be transformed. We believe that God is always working through us to bring about change in others and in ourselves. Jesus is the role model for that. He came into the world and transformed it by showing us a new way to look and see. There is great power in transformation just as there is great power in how we can change the world through God's love. Essential to this transformation is the realization that there really is nothing that can separate us from the love of God: "For I am convinced that neither death nor life, neither angels nor demons, neither the present nor the future, nor any powers, neither height nor depth, nor anything else in all creation, will be able to separate us from the love of God that is in Christ Jesus our Lord" (Rom. 8:38–39).

Transformation is a process. Events in life, both positive and negative, can be transforming. It seems, though, that we are more transformed by the negative challenges in life than by the positive. When we overcome a major challenge, we may be transformed by that challenge. For example, one friend told me that on her first long hiking trip, she was challenged by the climbing they had to do. At one point, she was ready to give up but was convinced to go on. Through tears and pain and praying, she was finally able to finish the hike. Afterward, she realized that her relationship with God had changed, that her faith was much stronger as a result of her persevering. This new way of being with God led her to a deeper relationship with God, one more meaningful for her. The new way of approaching life that she had found under duress continues to help her, many years later, as she faces other life challenges.

Being able to use whatever time one has left to the betterment of one's life, one's family, and one's relationship with God is transformational both for the patient, for the patient's family and for those close to the patient. Forgiving and being forgiven are transformational moments because we are able to see something from a new angle — as happened with the man who stole the candy bar. He was transformed when he had forgiven himself. He was no longer afraid to die. He was at peace with himself and with God. Enabling these moments for those who are dying is priceless and filled with grace.

Transformation for Family Members

I have watched many family members face their loved one who was dying with great trepidation and fear, not knowing what to say or how to say it. Not knowing whether or not to bring up unresolved issues for fear of upsetting the patient, nor knowing whether it was okay to seek forgiveness or offer it. In these situations you can facilitate the possibility of family members and the patient finding a new way for them to be with each other. Doing a life review with the patients and/or the patient's family can be transforming, as discussed in chapter 6. Helping families to deal with conflict surfaced by their loved one's dying can also lead to transformation. The two sisters who fought over their mother's wishes were transformed: they not only came together at their mother's bedside, but also were willing to talk with their congregation about what happened and how they were able to move from fighting to being with their mother as she died. They were able to see each other and their mother in a new way. Being with them and watching as they talked to the congregation about their experience brought a new understanding to me of how we can be transformed by events that occur in our lives. They owned both their fighting and their willingness to listen to each other's pain and love for their mother. And they talked about how important it was for them to have each other and to have God with them at the bedside as their mother died. We are transformed by the grace received when we are willing to put our love and our relationship on the line and in God's hands.

Transformation for Congregations

A group of men find a new way when none is seen. They know that if they can get to see this man who has healed so many that their friend too will be healed. So they try to get in, but there are too many people — so many in fact, that they are already standing around the outside of the house hoping to find their own way to get inside. These loyal friends look for another way — a new way — to get in. One of them suggests that they find a way to open the thatched roof and lower their friend who is in need of healing. So they climb onto the roof, bringing with them their friend who can only encourage them. They have to lift him and move him, for he is a paralytic and cannot assist in their plan. They find a place in the roof that amazingly is near where they know the one who heals is sitting. They open a place in the roof and lower their friend down on his mat. I can imagine them looking through the hole in the roof, wondering what this man will do when he sees their friend. They expect nothing for themselves. They are doing this for their friend. Their faith that Jesus could heal their friend enabled them as a community to move outside of themselves. They were transformed by their faith. The writer of Mark says that "when Jesus saw their faith, he said to the paralyzed man, 'Son, your sins are forgiven'" (Mark 2:5). So not only was the paralytic healed because of the faith of his friends, but the men were also transformed. Jesus saw that they understood what he was trying to teach them: to turn to God and not be encumbered with the way things had been. These men were no longer self-occupied. As I mentioned in chapter 8, we tend not to notice the miracles that occur around us in community when we reach out to help others. These men brought about a miracle when they transcended themselves. They found a new way and were, therefore, transformed.

Congregations can learn a great deal from these friends who looked for another way, a new way to help their friend. Coming out of ourselves to help others can enable us to see differently. Remember the families that supported each other in the ICU waiting room? They were a thrown-together community who had prayed together, laughed together, and cried together. In their own pain they were able to reach out to others in pain to help them. Months after this happened, the son of the man who was critically ill stopped by my office. The man had made it through and was about to come home from rehab. As we talked, the son mentioned the time spent in the waiting room and how he had been forever changed by the kindness that the other families had shown him and his mother. He said that he had gone to the funerals of the other two patients, who did not survive, and now found himself spending time with those families. He said that he felt that his heart was more open to them than it had ever been with anyone outside of his family. He found himself wanting to help others who had to spend long hours in the ICU waiting room. He said that it had been on his heart since he had felt the love of God through the other families that were there with him and his mother, and he had been praying about it. He wanted to know how he could help. He wanted to go outside of himself to help the "other" who was going through a difficult time. He had been transformed.

This is not an unusual case. Those who have been through a transformational experience often want to "give back" and help others who may be in a similar situation.

Our commitment as Christians is to be in community and to help those who are in need of being brought to Jesus for healing. Our actions can be transforming for someone else, just as the paralytic was transformed because of the faith of his friends. Our faith can be used in this positive way to help by being a healing presence. Our community is thus transformed as we move outside of ourselves to those in need.

Transformation for You, the Clergyperson

As I mentioned above, in leading clergy workshops using the Prayerful Discernment Process, one of the points for discussion I raise is this: "If you have concerns, imagine how your congregants feel. They believe that you have a closer relationship with God than they have." As we would continue the discussion there would be a clear shift. A transformation would begin to take root with the realization that they could make a difference for their congregations by having those "hard to have" conversations while people were healthy. As they learned about how they could be helpful to their congregants by being the provider of "clear and convincing evidence," or encouraging a conversation about health care proxies with families, or even giving some tips on how to preach about death and dying, they would see a "new way" of looking at their own fears of talking about death and dying. Additionally, a question about how many times they had preached about death, even on Good Friday, was likewise transformational as they admitted that they really did avoid talking about death and dying. This brought about a reconceptualization of this aspect of their ministry. This was God's transforming power at work.

We can make an incredible difference for those whom we serve as well as for ourselves by looking at new ways to approach these conversations, new ways to talk about the "nuts and bolts" of completing advance directives, new ways of facilitating life reviews and reconciliations, new ways of understanding that there is a need for you to just be present. You don't have to have the answers. You are, in a sense, the answer already. You are representing the One who brings about the ultimate transformation: from this life to life everlasting. You represent God's free gifts of love, forgiveness, reconciliation, and acceptance. By your being present at a deathbed, you are reminding those present that God too is present. Even in death, God does not desert us; your presence reminds them that our faith is not in vain. God transforms us even unto death — transforms not only the one who is dying, but all of those who are present to that death. Love is the greatest form of transformation. We cannot help but be transformed by love, and the love that you offer to those whom you serve will not only transform them, it will transform you as you come to see death in a new way: death is a part of life and dying is a part of living. Death is *not* the final word. New life through Jesus Christ is the final word.

Appendix 1

State-Specific Websites for Information about Advance Directives

Please note: some of these sites are sponsored by state governments, some by state associations, and some by state bar associations. Most give information about advance directives in their state, but a few have only the advance directive forms. You can also go to *www.caringinfo.org/stateaddownload* to get a copy of the advance directive form that is acceptable in each state. You will also find this information on the website *www.deathisnottheenemy.com*.

Alabama
www.medicaid.alabama.gov/resources/advance_directives.aspx?tab=5
or: *www.alaha.org/resources.aspx?id=33&terms=advance+directives*

Alaska
www.epi.hss.state.ak.us/pubs/guide/guide_16.htm

Arizona
www.azsos.gov/adv_dir/ADR/forms.htm

Arkansas
www.arkbar.com/whats_new/Advance%20Directive%20Information%20-%20 for%20ABA.pdf

California
www.iha4health.org/default.aspx/MenuItemID/266/MenuGroup/_Home.htm

Colorado
www.cdphe.state.co.us/em/Operations/AdvanceDirectives/index.html

Connecticut
www.ct.gov/ag/lib/ag/health/yourrightstomakehealthcaredecisions2006version.pdf

Delaware
www.dhss.delaware.gov/dhss/dsaapd/advance.html

Florida
www.floridahealthfinder.gov/reports-guides/end-life-issues.shtml

Georgia
Go to *www.aging.dhr.georgia.gov/* and search for "advance directive"

125

Hawaii
*http://hawaii.gov/health/disability-services/neurotrauma/key-services-health.html#
adirective*

Idaho
*www.idahocareline.org/eLibrary/Living%20Wills%20and%20Natural%20Death
%20Act.html*

Illinois
www.idph.state.il.us/public/books/advdir4.htm

Indiana
www.caringinfo.org/userfiles/File/Indiana.pdf

Iowa
www.nupplegal.com/iowa-power-health.html

Kansas
www.agingkansas.org/Publications/resource_guide/008.htm

Kentucky
www.florence-ky.gov/docs/fire/ky_living_will.pdf

Louisiana
http://goea.louisiana.gov/docs/LA01.pdf

Maine
www.maine.gov/dhhs/oes/resource/rit2chew.htm

Maryland
www.michigan.gov/mdch/0,1607,7-132-2941_4868_41752—,00.html

Massachusetts
*www.massmed.org/AM/Template.cfm?Section=Home&TEMPLATE=/CM/
HTMLDisplay.cfm&CONTENTID=10737*

Michigan
www.michbar.org/elderlaw/adpamphlet.cfm

Minnesota
www.revisor.leg.state.mn.us/statutes/?id=145C

Mississippi
http://unite.msdh.state.ms.us/msdhsite/_static/resources/75.pdf

Missouri
www.kcmba.org/PublicService/advdir.htm

Montana
www.doj.mt.gov/consumer/consumer/advancedirectives.asp

Nebraska
www.hhs.state.ne.us/ags/advdir.htm

Nevada
www.unr.edu/ncehp/ADs.html

New Hampshire
*www.healthynh.com/fhc/initiatives/performance/eol/ACPG%202007%20
revisions.pdf*

New Jersey
www.state.nj.us/health/healthfacilities/documents/ltc/advance_directives.pdf

New Mexico
www.nmaging.state.nm.us/AHCD.html

New York
www.oag.state.ny.us/media_center/2005/jan/jan31b_05.html

North Carolina
www.secretary.state.nc.us/ahcdr/

North Dakota
www.nd.gov/dhs/info/pubs/docs/aging/aging-healthcare-directives-guide.pdf

Ohio
http://olrs.ohio.gov/asp/olrs_AdvanceDirect.asp

Oklahoma
www.oag.state.ok.us/oagweb.nsf/AdvanceDirective

Oregon
http://egov.oregon.gov/DCBS/SHIBA/advanced_directives.shtml

Pennsylvania
*www.pamedsoc.org/MainMenuCategories/Government/LawsAffectingPhysicians/
AdvanceDirectives/Act169facts.aspx*

Rhode Island
www.health.state.ri.us/hsr/directives.php

South Carolina
www.aging.sc.gov/seniors/AdvanceDirectives/

South Dakota
www.rcrh.org/Services/Patient/AdvancedDirectives.asp

Tennessee
http://health.state.tn.us/AdvanceDirectives/index.htm

Texas
www.dshs.state.tx.us/alzheimers/legal.shtm

Utah
www.hsdaas.utah.gov/advance_directives.htm

Vermont
www.vtpa.org/Advance_Directive.html

Virginia
www.vda.virginia.gov/advmedir.asp

Washington
www.wsma.org/patient_resources/advance-directives-qa.cfm

West Virginia
www.wvbar.org/barinfo/lawyer/will2.htm

Wisconsin
http://dhs.wisconsin.gov/forms/AdvDirectives/

Wyoming
www.health.wyo.gov/aging/forms.html

Appendix 2

Denominational Links to End-of-Life Issues and Other Denominational Resources

American Baptist Church
www.abc-usa.org/Resources/resol/death.htm

Episcopal Church
episcopalfoundation.org/library/Planned%20Giving%20booklets

"Establish Principles with Regard to the Prolongation of Life"
http://fn.org/2005/03/msg00254.html

Evangelical Lutheran Churches in America
www.elca.org/What-We-Believe/Social-Issues/Messages/End-of-Life-Decisions.aspx

The Lutheran Church — Missouri Synod
www.lcms.org/pages/internal.asp?NavID=14625

Presbyterian Church USA
www.pcusa.org/theologyandworship/science/end.htm

United Church of Christ
www.ucc.org/science/pdf/microsoft-word-end-of-life-care-with-theological-ethical-spiritual-resources.pdf

> "Making End of Life Decisions: UCC Perspectives"
> *www.deathisnottheenemy.com/media/media-115462.pdf*

United Methodist Church
www.umc.org/site/c.lwL4KnN1LtH/b.2247677/k.5AEE/Death_and_Dying_Overview.htm

Unitarian Universalist
As with so many personal issues, UUs leave a lot of freedom to private conscience in making end-of-life decisions. There are a few formal statements (adopted by vote at the General Assemblies):

> "The Right to Die with Dignity"
> *www.uua.org/socialjustice/socialjustice/statements/14486.shtml*

"The Legality of Living Wills"
www.uua.org/socialjustice/socialjustice/statements/20279.shtml

"Development of Hospices"
www.uua.org/socialjustice/socialjustice/statements/20275.shtml

Interfaith Resources

Compassion Sabbath (*www.practicalbioethics.org.*) is an interfaith initiative to help clergy and congregations minister to seriously ill and dying people.

Florida statewide hospice clergy end-of-life education enhancement project: *www.hospicefoundation.org/professionalEducation/clergyEducation/.*

Hawaii: *End-of-Life Choices and the Ministry of Caregiving:*
A handbook of educational activities and resources for churches and temples: *www.hawaii.edu/aging/.*

New York: Hospice and Palliative Care of St. Lawrence Valley, New York. *http://seriousillness.org/slc/resources/clergy.php.*

Other Resources

Books with Denominational Information

Episcopal
Cynthia B. Cohen. *Faithful Living, Faithful Dying: Anglican Reflections on End of Life Care.* End of Life Task Force of the Standing Commission on National Concerns, published by Morehouse Publishing, 2000.

Methodist
Edwin R. DuBose. "Religious Beliefs and Healthcare Decisions: The United Methodist Tradition." In *Religious Traditions and Healthcare Decisions.* Chicago: Park Ridge Center, 2003.

UUA
David John Doukas and William Reichel. *Planning for Uncertainty: Living Wills and Other Advance Directives for You and Your Family.* 2nd ed. Baltimore: Johns Hopkins University Press, 2007. A practical guide to help individuals make end-of-life decisions and communicate them to health care providers, family members, and other loved ones. Dr. William Reichel is a member of Towson Unitarian Universalist Church in Lutherville, Maryland.

United Church of Christ
Making End-of-Life Decisions: UCC Perspectives on End of Life Care. Ed. Rev. Julie Ruth Harley. Cleveland: UCC Council for Health and Human Service Ministries, 1997. This booklet is a study guide that seeks to address "specific moral issues at the

end of life" and covers a diversity of topics, including overcoming the fear of dying, living wills and health care proxies, and making health care decisions for others. Also included are relevant church resolutions, a glossary of terms, and a bibliography of other available resources. To obtain a free copy, go to *www.deathisnottheenemy.com*.

Articles

Methodist: James R. Thobaben. "A United Methodist Approach to End-of-Life Decisions: Intentional Ambiguity or Ambiguous Intentions." *Christian Bioethics* 3, no. 3 (1997): 222–48.

Appendix 3

Advance Directives and End-of-Life Web Resources

The descriptions of these websites come from the websites themselves. I am not recommending any of these sites. They are for your information. You will also find this list on the website.

The following two websites are for general information about advance directives:

National Institutes of Health: *www.nlm.nih.gov/medlineplus/advancedirectives.html*

National Cancer Institute: *www.cancer.gov/cancertopics/factsheet/support/advance-directives*

Booklets on Advance Directives

Caring Conversations
Center for Practical Bioethics
www.practicalbioethics.org/cpb.aspx?pgID=986

Finding Your Way
Sacramento Health Care Decisions
www.sachealthdecisions.org/finding.html

Five Wishes
www.agingwithdignity.org/5wishes.html

Respecting Choices
An advance care planning system from Gundersen Lutheran Medical Foundation
www.respectingchoices.org/

Ethical Wills
Offers a way to leave your legacy by writing down your values and beliefs.
www.ethicalwill.com

Other Helpful State Websites

California Department of Developmental Services, Consumer Advisory Committee, has developed plain language pictorial publications and DVDs that encourage self-direction and personal choice. The *Thinking Ahead Workbook* is also able to be downloaded. *www.dds.ca.gov/consumercorner/publications.cfm*

132

California Coalition for Compassionate Care is a statewide partnership of more than sixty organizations dedicated to advancement of palliative medicine and end-of-life care. It provides information about end-of-life decision making, legislation, and forms. A downloadable copy of the *Thinking Ahead Workbook* and facilitator guidelines are available. *www.finalchoices.org*

The Complete Life is a two-part curriculum developed as part of a larger effort to improve end-of-life care in Hawaii. Designed specifically for faith communities but utilized among caregivers, professionals, and paraprofessionals working in the field of aging.
www.kokuamau.org/resources/complete-life-course

Massachusetts Commission on End of Life Care
www.endoflifecommission.org/end_pages/about.htm

Nebraska Coalition for Compassionate Care
www.nebrccc.org/educational_guide.htm

Grand Island, Nebraska's Respect My Wishes
Nebraska: *www.respectmywishes.org/professionals/clergy.html*

Other Helpful Websites

American Academy of Hospice and Palliative Care:
www.aahpm.org

American Bar Association Commission on Law and Aging:
www.abanet.org/aging

Caring Connections: National Hospice and Palliative Care Organization committed to improving care at the end of life.
www.caringinfo.org

Center for Healthcare Decisions: Dedicated to advancing healthcare that is fair and affordable and that reflects the priorities of an informed public.
www.chcd.org/index.html

Completing a Life is a Web-based resource for taking charge, finding comfort, and reaching closure. It features an interactive CD-ROM and website inviting patients and families to learn about the practical, emotional, spiritual, and medical issues faced by those dealing with advanced illness.
http://commtechlab.msu.edu/sites/completingalife/index.html

Death and Dying Resource Guide from Forbes.com:
www.forbes.com/2004/08/18/cx_mh_0818deathresources.html.

Dying Well: Dr. Ira Byock's website has resources for people facing life-limiting illness, their families, and their professional caregivers.
www.dyingwell.com

Growth House, Inc., provides a portal to resources for life-threatening illness and end-of-life care. Their primary mission is to improve the quality of compassionate care for people who are dying. They do this through public education and global professional collaboration. Their search engine gives you access to a comprehensive collection of reviewed resources for end-of-life care.
www.growthhouse.org/

The Hastings Center is a nonpartisan research institution dedicated to bioethics and the public interest since 1969.
www.thehastingscenter.org

Hospice Foundation of America exists to help those who cope personally or professionally with terminal illness, death, and the process of grief and bereavement.
www.hospicefoundation.org

Library and Information Services, Kennedy Institute of Ethics, Georgetown University:
http://bioethics.georgetown.edu/nrc/resources/AdvanceDirectives.htm

National Center for Ethics in Health Care examines questions about ethical health care practices. It educates VA staff and leaders about health care ethics.
www.va.gov/vhaethics

National Hospice and Palliative Care Organization provides a search for hospice and palliative care, as well as statistics, resources, and information.
www.nhpco.org

OnOurOwnTerms is Bill Moyers's website, which came out of the series that he did for PBS on end of life and the issues surrounding death and dying.
www.pbs.org/wnet/onourownterms

The Palliative Care Policy Center offers expert support to hospitals, nursing homes, health systems, hospices, and other organizations that serve individuals nearing the end of life.
www.medicaring.org

Physician Orders for Life-Sustaining Treatment (POLST) program is designed to improve the quality of care people receive at the end of life. It is based on effective communication of patient wishes, documentation of medical orders on a brightly colored form, and a promise by health care professionals to honor these wishes.
http://www.ohsu.edu/ethics/polst

Supportive Care of the Dying: A Coalition for Compassionate Care is a nonprofit coalition committed to bringing about cultural change regarding pain and symptom management and relief of suffering for persons living with and affected by life-threatening illness.
www.careofdying.org

Appendix 4

Prayerful Discernment Process for Congregational Use

When your congregants arrive, they will probably be nervous. If you can, have soft drinks and water (not caffeine) available, and perhaps some cookies, that might help ease things up. Be sure to have lots of paper, pens, tissues, and water on the tables already. (You will find a PowerPoint version of this process at *www.deathisnottheenemy.com*.)

As with clergy, I suggest that some ground rules be set before beginning this process:

- Turn off cell phones.

- Stay present. In other words, if you finish before others, do not start reading a book or doing needlework. Stay in the moment.

- Try not to talk during the process. It can be distracting for others and for you. If you are not sure what a question means, answer it as best you can.

- When you are finished, put your pen down to signal that you are done, and we can move onto the next question.

- If you cannot answer a question, that is okay.

- There are no "right" or "wrong" answers, only your answers.

- No one will see your answers. They are for you only — you do not have to share them, unless you want to.

Today we are going to be talking about our living and our dying. You may feel strong emotions in response to the questions I am going to be asking. That is okay and is to be expected. Be aware of why

135

you are feeling what you are feeling and make a note about it for yourself. If you need to, take a deep breath, drink some water, and allow yourself to feel what you are feeling. I will be here with you and so will God.

Read aloud Psalm 139:1–18, 23–24.

Opening Prayer

Holy One, we come here this day and thank You for all that You have given us. You have called us to serve You and we do so humbly knowing that You love us just as we are and for who we are.

Holy God, we come together this day to talk about our living and our dying. This is scary for most of us so we are trusting in You to hold us as we explore our hopes, our fears, our mortality. Help us to remember that You are here with us and will never desert us.

Help us always to remember that there is nothing that we cannot accomplish when we include You in every aspect of our lives. Amen.

Reflection

- Take a few minutes to reflect on who you are and what is important to you. Think about what you have accomplished and what you still want to do. Think about the most important aspect of yourself (for example, your body, your mind) — what is it that makes you, you?

- What do you hope that others will see as your legacy?

- What do you hope people will say about you after you have died?

- What do you think people will say about you after you have died?

- Consider how you would like to die. For example, do you see yourself in a hospital or at home or someplace else?

- Is your death sudden or is it lingering?

- Why is it important to you whether it is sudden or lingering?

- Who do you want present with you while you are dying?

- Who do you *not* want present with you while you are dying?

- Are there things you want to make sure that you say to particular people? Give some examples, if you wish.

- Do you have a bottom line in terms of what you would physically or mentally need or want to be able to do in order for your life to have meaning for you? What is that bottom line?

- What if that bottom line is reached. Do you want extraordinary measures used to keep you alive no matter what?

- Where does your belief system fit into your living and your dying?

- Where is God in your dying? Where do you see God — or maybe you don't see God?

- Do you think that God would want you to stay alive at all costs, no matter what?

- Have you talked with your family about your wishes? If the answer is "no," Why not?

- Have you talked with a clergyperson about your wishes? If the answer is "no," Why not?

- Have you talked with your doctor about your wishes? If the answer is "no," why not?

- What is your greatest fear about dying?

Discuss the process, reminding the participants that they do not have to share their answers if they don't want to.

- How did it feel to be asked these questions?

- How did you feel as you wrote your responses to them?

- Did any of your answers surprise you?

- Did you learn anything about yourself that you didn't already know?

- What bothers you the most about your death?

- Are you afraid of death?

- Are you afraid of the dying process?

- Do you think that you can talk with your family members about your fears and concerns regarding your dying and your death?

- Are you going to have these conversations with your family? If not, why not?

Read aloud Psalm 139:1–18, 23–24.

Closing Prayer

Holy God, this has been a difficult time for some of us. It has forced us to face our humanness in a way that is not necessarily comfortable for us. Thank you for being present with us and helping us to begin to look at our living and our dying. Remind us when we are fearful of death that You will be there with us each step of the way. Help us as we begin to have these discussions with our family members. Let Your love and presence be felt in each person who explores their fears, their concerns, and their mortality. Help us to always to remember that through our faith in You, we can live and we can die. We pray these prayers with the assurance of the love and compassion that your Son, Jesus Christ, has shown to us throughout our lives. We know that Jesus will be there to welcome our souls into God's presence. Amen.

After the process is completed, you might want to have available blank copies of the form your state uses for advance directives. Distribute them and encourage the participants to complete them. If you are willing, offer to "stop by" to help them if they feel that they need your support in conversations with family members.

Appendix 5

Materials and Resources
for Use with Congregations

Interfaith Dialogues for End of Life Ministry: A manual for building successful, faith-based ministries to address death, dying, and life at the end of life. A Project of the Community State Partnership, the Maine Consortium for Palliative Care and Hospice, and the Maine Council of Churches. Retrieved January 15, 2008. Go online to *www.mainehospicecouncil.org/resources/publications.htm* and look for "Interfaith Dialogues for End of Life Ministry."

The Maine Council of Churches Dialogues list

• To Accept the Things We Cannot Change: The Spirituality of Death and Dying (meaning and death, religious traditions, rituals, spiritual growth)

• Caring for a Loved One with a Life Threatening Illness (primary caregivers, respite, support groups, chronic illness)

• The Effects of Life Threatening Illness on the Family System (communication, family dynamics, stress, emotions, support)

• Grief and Bereavement (the process of grieving, reactions to loss, styles of grieving, mourning rituals, red flags, signs of unhealthy grief)

• Courage to Change the Things We Can: Decision Making at the End of Life (advance directives, estate planning, power of attorney, advance care planning, decisions in the critical care unit)

- How We Die (basic physiology and disease processes, signs and symptoms of approaching death, personal death awareness)

- Providing Freedom from Pain: Palliative Care and Hospice (types of pain, medication options, complementary therapies, hospice philosophy, palliative care)

- How Can I Help? (hospice volunteering, lay ministry, organ donation, community outreach, prayer care)

- To Accept the Things We Cannot Change: The Spirituality of Death and Dying — Part II (meaning and death, religious traditions, rituals, spiritual growth)

- The High Cost of Dying (meaning and death, religious traditions, rituals, spiritual growth, reimbursement, navigating the health care system)

- The Details of Dying (calling hours, funeral and memorial services, cremation, other options, legal issues, organ donation)

EndLink is an Internet-based end-of-life care education program established by the Robert H. Lurie Comprehensive Cancer Center of Northwestern University. It lists twelve activities to encourage participation of faith communities in end-of-life care. See *http://endlink.lurie.northwestern.edu/more_about/communities.cfm*.

1. Providing ongoing education of members on beliefs about meaning of life, suffering, illness, healing, dying and death, and afterlife.

2. Raising awareness about fundamental religious values vis-à-vis medicine.

3. Offering educational forums on specific issues related to end of life such as advanced directives, funeral and burial customs, legal matters and estate planning, and hospice care.

4. Advocating within the medical system respect for religious beliefs, practices, and prohibitions as well as stressing the importance of spiritual care at the end of life.

5. Helping members clarify specific goals of medical care that are in keeping with religious beliefs and values.

6. Assisting patients and families with difficult decisions regarding the direction of medical treatment and ethical dilemmas about withdrawal of life support, artificial nutrition, use of antibiotics, etc.

7. Providing spiritual care and counseling to patients who are terminally ill and to their families.

8. Mediating divine presence and affirming value and personhood.

9. Providing assistance in sustaining religious practices and rituals for patients in the hospital or unable to leave home.

10. Providing practical assistance such as respite for caregivers, meals, running errands, and housekeeping.

11. Ensuring proper disposition and treatment of the body at the time of death and conducting funerals, memorial services, and burial rites.

12. Offering bereavement counseling and grief support groups.

The Duke Institute on Care at the End of Life is creating a Toolkit for Faith Communities to help them address end-of-life issues. It was in process at the time of the creation of this list. See *www.iceol.duke.edu/about/programs/toolkit.html.*

Florida Statewide Hospice Clergy End-of-Life Education Enhancement Project. *www.hospicefoundation.org/professionalEducation/ clergyEducation/.*

Hawaii. *The Complete Life* is a two-part curriculum developed as part of a larger effort to improve end-of-life care in Hawaii. Designed specifically for faith communities. *www.hawaii.edu/aging/elife.htm.*

Respect My Wishes Information and Resource Guide for Grand Island, Nebraska, for clergy *www.respectmywishes.org/professionals/clergy.html.*

Compassion Sabbath resources: You will find this information on the website (*www.deathisnottheenemy.com*).

Appendix 6

Book Suggestions on Grieving and Rituals

Books on Anticipatory Grieving and Grieving in General

Attig, Thomas. *How We Grieve: Relearning the World.* New York: Oxford University Press, 1996.

Bennett, Paul. *Loving Grief.* Burdett, N.Y.: Larson, 2009.

Boss, Pauline. *Ambiguous Loss: Learning to Live with Unresolved Grief.* Cambridge, Mass.: Harvard University Press, 2000.

————. *Loss, Trauma, and Resilience: Therapeutic Work with Ambiguous Loss.* New York: W. W. Norton, 2006.

Doka, Kenneth J. *Living with Grief: At Work, at School, at Worship.* Washington, D.C.: Hospice Foundation of America, 1999.

————. *Living with Grief: Who We Are, How We Grieve.* Washington, D.C.: Hospice Foundation of America, 1998.

Garrett, Greg. *Stories from the Edge: A Theology of Grief.* Louisville: Westminster John Knox, 2008.

Koven, Mara, and Liz Pearl, eds. *Mourning Has Broken: A Collection of Creative Writing about Grief and Healing.* Toronto: KOPE Associates, 2006.

Mitchell, Kenneth R., and Herbert Anderson. *All Our Losses, All Our Griefs: Resources for Pastoral Care.* Louisville: Westminster John Knox Press, 1983.

VanDuivendyk, Tim P. *The Unwanted Gift of Grief: A Ministry Approach.* New York: Haworth Pastoral Press, 2006.

Zurheide, Jeffry R. *When Faith Is Tested.* Minneapolis: Augsburg Fortress, 1997.

Rituals for the End of Life

Anderson, Megory. *Sacred Dying: Creating Rituals for Embracing the End of Life.* New York: Marlowe, 2004.

Irish, Donald P., Kathleen F. Lundquist, and Vivian Jenkins Nelsen. *Ethnic Variations in Dying, Death, and Grief: Diversity in Universality.* Washington, D.C.: Taylor & Francis, 1993.

Toole, Mary M. *Handbook for Chaplains: Comfort My People.* New York and Mahwah, N.J.: Paulist Press, 2006.

York, Sarah. *Remembering Well: Rituals for Celebrating Life and Mourning Death.* San Francisco: Jossey-Bass, 2000.

Appendix 7

Sample Sermon:
A Chaplain's Prayer

Originally preached by
the Rev. Dr. Martha R. Jacobs
April 1997

Psalm 139:1–18, 23–24; Luke 12:35–39

I want to begin today by admitting that I am nervous about this sermon, which I have entitled "A Chaplain's Prayer," because I am going to be talking about end-of-life issues — not an easy topic to preach about or to hear about. Death and end-of-life issues are not often raised from the pulpit, except in terms of living a so-called "good life" so that we will be acceptable servants of God and will be able to enter heaven.

As a hospital chaplain, however, I am finding it difficult to be quiet about a missing link that I encounter all too often, namely the lack of conversation between parents and children, spouse and spouse, patient and doctor, and patient and pastor.

These are conversations we need to have about how we want to be medically treated as we near the end of our life.

Luke describes in his Gospel the love and healing power of Jesus. As we know, there are all kinds of healing. As we near the end of our life, our focus changes from healing of body to healing of spirit. Not only do we concern ourselves with our own spiritual healing, but also we concern ourselves with our loved ones and the impact of our death on them. I have been in too many situations where families are arguing with each other about what invasive procedures their mom or dad would have wanted to keep them alive. At the time a family should be coming together for healing, they are split apart. These situations do not allow God's love and healing to be present.

We need to be prepared because our physical being is vulnerable. It is the part of us that will one day fail us. Whether it be due to old age, tragic accident, or illness, we are all eventually going to die. That is one thing we all have in common. While we may not have a say in when that happens, I believe we do have a mandate from God to be ready for our death, both spiritually and physically. We have an obligation while we are still alive to deal with the inevitable. And in some ways, we do deal with our death. We deal with it in terms of how we live our lives. We live our lives by loving our neighbor as we love ourselves. We try our best to serve God as we believe we should. We open our hearts and minds to God's will for us. We search our hearts and seek to do the best we can do, while honoring God and the body and mind we have been given in order to serve God.

We worry about who is going to get our material wealth. How will we divide our material wealth among our loved ones? And so, we prepare for our deaths in other ways. We write wills; we tell our children our history, hoping that they will carry it with them and tell their children. We do our best to prepare for our death and to live the life God wants us to live. And yet there is an important part of our future that we neglect: a missing link that can make the difference between a peaceful, dignified death and one fraught with difficulties for you and your family. The consequences of that missing link can be observed in the hospital all too often. Families do not communicate to each other their wishes about end-of-life health care. The Supreme Court of the United States has tried to help us in this area.

In April of 1975, a twenty-one-year-old woman named Karen Ann Quinlin, for reasons that were never fully determined, ceased breathing for at least two fifteen-minute periods. As a result she suffered severe brain damage and was in what is called in a persistent vegetative state. She had no cognitive function. Her parents went to court to have the respirator disconnected so that their daughter could die. The Supreme Court of New Jersey took up the case, and ruled that Karen could be removed from life support. The story goes that she was in a Catholic hospital and the nurses, knowing the ruling was coming, had weaned Karen off the respirator, so when the time came to remove her from it, she was able to breath on her own. She remained in this vegetative state for another ten years before she finally died.

In the 1980s a young woman named Nancy Cruzan was in a terrible car crash that left her in a permanent vegetative state. She was breathing on her own and was receiving artificial nutrition and hydration. After many years, it became obvious that she too would never awaken. Her parents wanted the tube feedings that were keeping her alive to be discontinued. The hospital said no. Nancy's parents went to court. The case eventually wended its way to the U.S. Supreme Court, which ruled that individuals have a right to self-determination. And so advance directives were born in 1990, when the New York State legislature responded to the Supreme Court ruling by upholding patient rights through the use of a health care agent.

In New York State, if you do not have a health care agent and are incapable of speaking for yourself, doctors are required to do everything they can to keep you alive, no matter what your quality of life might be. Let me repeat that. In New York State, if you do not have a health care agent and are incapable of speaking for yourself, doctors are required to do everything they can to keep you alive, no matter what your quality of life might be. A living will, which many people have, is not enough in New York. You must appoint a health care agent in addition to drafting a living will in order for your wishes to be honored. A health care proxy form is as important as your will, which states your wishes for your property and money. Why do we worry about material objects, our money and our property, and not about how our bodies are to be handled as we near the end of our life?

I want to share two different family stories with you today. These are true stories; the names have been changed to ensure confidentiality. I ask you to imagine yourself in these situations. Tom was fifty-five years old. He had been diagnosed with lung cancer eighteen months before his current admission to the hospital. He had been in the hospital several times previously, but this was his most difficult hospitalization because his disease had progressed. His chances of leaving the hospital were very slight. Shortly after his admission, Tom lapsed into a coma. To keep him breathing, it was necessary to intubate him so that a machine could do the breathing for him. Without the help of this machine, Tom would die in a very short time. Tom's wife and family were approached by the doctor and asked whether Tom had expressed his wishes concerning life support and whether he had a health care agent. Tom's wife said that they had never discussed life support because they did not want to upset the children. She also thought it would upset Tom too much to talk about it. She did not know what his wishes were, but she knew in her heart that he would not want to be kept alive by machines. What Tom's wife knew in her heart was not enough. By law, the doctor had no choice. Tom was put on a respirator. Tom's wife asked to speak with me. She said that she did not understand why he was put on a respirator. Why couldn't they just let him go in peace?

She was very upset, as were his children. She talked about how much Tom had loved life and loved God and worked his whole life to serve God and others. She wanted to know why God was doing this to her husband. Why was God now making him suffer after he had been so faithful? She was angry with God. She believed that God should have taken care of Tom in such a way that he would not have to be kept alive by machines. Tom died several days later after developing complications. While he was not in pain, his life was prolonged by machines because he did not appoint someone to be his health care agent.

Harriet was an eighty-five-year-old woman who had been relatively healthy for most of her life. She suffered a stroke that left her physically immobilized, yet her mind was intact.

She told her grandson that she was ready and wanted to die. Her grandson was beside himself, as Harriet had raised him from childhood. He did not know what to do. Despite his grandmother being competent, he was not sure whether she really understood her request to be allowed to die. Harriet remembered that she had completed a health care proxy form, which was obtained from her home. Her proxy form very clearly stated her wishes. Her grandson was greatly relieved when he realized that when she was healthy she had stated that she did not want extraordinary measures taken if she had no reasonable expectation for recovery. The proxy form assured him that she understood what she was asking for. She went into the hospital's hospice program and was allowed to die with dignity, in comfort and peace. And her family was able to concentrate on Harriet and their final days with her. Unfortunately, most of the families I deal with are in situations like Tom's. I wish more were like Harriet's.

I have shared these stories with you not to scare you, but to ask that you look within and consider what your wishes would be if something were to happen to you. What if you could not make your own decisions about your care? Who would you entrust to be your agent and make the decisions for you? What decisions would you want your agent to make? Would you want everything done for you, no matter what the outcome? If there was no reasonable expectation that you would recover, would you want nothing done, except comfort care? Would you want to donate organs? Would you want to be placed on a respirator if there was a chance you would survive? What if the chances were slim? What if whatever happens to you physically would cause you permanent damage that would drastically alter your quality of life?

All of these questions need to be answered by each one of us. They are hard questions. But imagine if you had not discussed these questions. Imagine your loved ones trying to figure out what your wishes would be. Instead of making the most of whatever time you have left, as was the case with Harriet's family, your loved ones would be trying to figure out what you would want. Then they would have to try to convince the hospital that these were your wishes. Lastly, your surviving loved ones would then wonder if they made the right decision. Did they make the decision you would have made? Is that what you want to happen?

A conversation on end-of-life issues is not an easy one to have, either with yourself or your loved ones. It is a conversation to have while you are healthy, whether you are young, like Karen Ann Quinlin and Nancy Cruzan, or old, whether or not you are currently facing a life-threatening illness. It is a conversation needed in this age of advanced technology when people can be kept alive for years, hooked up to machines. My suggestion, and one I give to all the community groups I talk with about health care proxies, is to invite your family and your extended family over for coffee and cake. Sit down at the kitchen table and give everyone in your household who is over the age of eighteen a blank copy of a health care proxy form. Then start talking about what your wishes are. It may be hard to begin the conversation, but it will be one of the most important conversations you and your family will ever have. These decisions should be made in a prayerful way, with God at the table with you.

God knows us intimately. God created us. God helps us to take care of ourselves and expects us to take responsibility for ourselves and how we live our lives. I believe God also expects us to take responsibility for how we allow our bodies to be treated as we near death. I have seen too many tragic situations to believe that God would want families to agonize over end-of-life health care for a loved one. These decisions need to be made in advance. Remember what a difference it made for Harriet and her family. She made her choices when she was healthy. Her grandson was able to accept them and helped her to die with dignity, which helped the family to prepare for and spend quality time with their loved one as she neared death. Remember Tom's family and their pain. They questioned God's presence and love at the very time they needed it most — but because there was no health care agent, they were bereft of God's comfort.

The health care proxy form is easy to complete. No lawyer is necessary. We will be getting together following today's service to talk more about and, hopefully, complete some proxy forms.

After you complete your proxy form, give a copy to your agent, to your doctor, and to your hospital, and keep one with your other important papers.

As you search your hearts and pray about writing your health care proxy form, my prayer for each of you is that you make your own decisions about how much you are to be treated when you are unable to make a decision for yourself. Be prepared for that time.

You owe it to yourself, to your family, and to your God.

Notes

Chapter 1: Why Are We Afraid to Die?

1. Pew Research Center for the People and the Press, "More Americans Discussing — and Planning — End-of-Life Treatment: Strong Public Support for Right to Die," January 5, 2006.

2. All biblical quotations, unless otherwise noted, are from Wayne A. Meeks, ed., *The HarperCollins Study Bible* (New York: HarperCollins, 1989).

3. Horatio Spafford, "It Is Well with My Soul," 1873.

4. Ernest Becker, *The Denial of Death* (New York: Simon and Schuster, 1973).

5. Daniel Callahan, "Death, Mourning and Medical Progress," *Perspectives in Biology and Medicine* 52, no. 1 (Winter 2009): 106.

6. Ibid., 109.

7. Ibid., 106.

8. Graham Shaw, *The Cost of Authority: Manipulation and Freedom in the New Testament* (Philadelphia: Fortress Press, 1982), 281.

9. Ibid.

10. For a discussion of healed vs. cured, see chapter 4.

11. William Sloane Coffin, *Credo* (Louisville: Westminster John Knox Press, 2004), 168.

12. Ibid., 169.

Chapter 2: Legal Issues

1. I will be using the term "agent" to include surrogate, agent, or other term that refers to the person selected to represent the wishes of the patient.

2. Margaret Mohrmann, *Medicine as Ministry* (Cleveland: Pilgrim Press, 1995), 13.

3. Ibid., 16.

4. Callahan, "Death, Mourning and Medical Progress," 107.

5. *Union Pacific Railway Co v. Botsford,* 141 US 250, 251 (1891). This case involved a woman who did not want to submit to a surgical examination by her adversary as to the extent of her injury. The Supreme Court upheld her right to refuse the examination.

6. Phillip M. Kleespies, *Life and Death Decisions: Psychological and Ethical Considerations in End-of-Life Care* (Washington, D.C.: American Psychological Association, 2004), 34.

7. *Schloendorff v. Society of New York Hospital,* 211 NY 125, 105 NE 92 (1914).

8. J. Luce and A. Alpers, "End-of-life Care: What Do the American Courts Say?" *Critical Care Medicine* 29, no. 2 Suppl (2001): N41.

9. Lawrence O. Gostin, "Deciding Life and Death in the Courtroom: From Quinlan to Cruzan, Glucksberg and Vacco — A Brief History and Analysis of Constitutional Protection of the 'Right to Die,'" *Journal of the American Medical Association* 278, no. 18 (November 12, 1997): 1524.

10. Ibid.

11. Angela Fagerlin and Carl E. Schneider, "Enough: The Failure of the Living Will," *Hastings Center Report* 34, no. 2 (March–April 2004): 30–42.

12. Sean R. Morrison and Diane E. Meier, "High Rates of Advance Care Planning in New York City's Elderly Population," *Archives of Internal Medicine* 164 (December 13/27, 2004): 24–25.

13. Martha R. Jacobs, "The Importance of Advance Directives," *PlainView* 1, no. 6 (April 21, 2004), *www.plainviews.org/AR/c/v1n6pp.html.*

14. Joseph J. Fins, "Commentary: From Contract to Covenant in Advance Care Planning," *Journal of Law, Medicine, and Ethics* 27 (1999): 13.

15. Ibid., 16.

16. Thomas H. Murray and Bruce Jennings, "The Quest to Reform End of Life Care: Rethinking Assumptions and Setting New Directions," *Hastings Center Report Special Report* 35, n. 6 (2005): S56.

17. Physician Orders for Life-Sustaining Treatment (POLST) Paradigm, *www.ohsu.edu/ethics/polst/,* accessed February 27, 2009.

18. Ibid.

19. Ibid.

20. New York State Department of Health website: *www.nyhealth.gov/professionals/patients/patient_rights/most/frequently_asked_questions.htm,* accessed November 18, 2007.

21. University of Buffalo Center for Clinical Ethics and Humanities in Health Care, *http://wings.buffalo.edu/bioethics/oconnor1.html,* accessed November 18, 20/07.

22. Kleespies, *Life and Death Decisions,* 69.

Chaper 3: Medical Issues

1. For more information on this law, go to the Centers for Medicare and Medicaid Services, *www.cms.hhs.gov/HIPAAGenInfo/02_TheHIPAALawandRelated%20Information.asp#TopOfPage.*

2. Jane Gross, "Keeping Patients' Details Private, even from Kin," *New York Times,* July 3, 2007. *www.nytimes.com/2007/07/03/health/policy/03hipaa.html?th&emc=th.*

3. J. Wilson, "Health Insurance Portability and Accountability Act Privacy Rule Causes Ongoing Concerns Among Clinicians and Researchers," *Annals of Internal Medicine* 145, no. 4 (2006): 313–16.

4. Clinical information about CHF was taken, in part, from *www.medicinenet .com/congestive_heart_failure/article.htm*.

5. Portions taken from Lynne Ann DeSpelder and Albert Lee Strickland, *The Last Dance: Encountering Death and Dying*, 6th ed. (New York and Mountain View, Calif.: Mayfield, 1999), 181, and the *Merck Manual of Health and Aging*, *www.merck.com/pubs/mmanual_ha/sidebars/sb16_2.html*, accessed August 14, 2007.

6. Ibid., 181.

7. Kleespies, *Life and Death Decisions*, 56–57.

8. Charles Meyer, *A Good Death: Challenges, Choices and Care Options* (Mystic, Conn.: Twenty-Third Publications, 2000), 9.

9. Ibid., 9.

10. Gallup Institute, *Spiritual Beliefs and the Dying Process: A Report on the National Survey Conducted for the Nathan Cummings Foundation and Fetzer Institute* (Princeton, N.J.: Gallup Institute, 1997), 32.

11. K. E. Steinhauser et al., "Factors Considered Important at the End of Life by Patients, Family, Physicians and Other Care Providers," *Journal of the American Medical Association* 284, no. 19 (November 2000): 2476–82.

12. Kleespies, *Life and Death Decisions*, 63.

13. Ibid., 36.

14. Meyer, *A Good Death*, 17.

15. DeSpelder and Strickland, *The Last Dance*, 182.

16. Ibid., 205.

17. Dena S. Davis. "Old and Thin," *Second Opinion* 15 (November 1990): 26–32.

18. See the Hospice Foundation of America, *www.hospicefoundation.org/ endOfLifeInfo/documents/general_manual.pdf*, accessed August 18, 2006.

19. The Merck Manuals Online Medical Library, *www.merck.com/mmpe/sec16/ ch212/ch212d.html*, accessed on January 23, 2009.

20. "End of Life Care: An Ethical Overview," Center for Bioethics, University of Minnesota, *www.ahc.umn.edu/img/assets/26104/End_of_Life.pdf*, accessed January 16, 2008, 33.

21. James J. Walter, "Terminal Sedation: A Catholic Perspective," *Update* 18, no. 6, cited in David F. Kelly, *Medical Care at the End of Life: A Catholic Perspective* (Washington, D.C.: Georgetown University Press, 2006), 19.

Chapter 4: Miracles and Cures

1. David Noel Freedman, ed., *The Anchor Bible Dictionary*, vol. 2, D-G (New York: Doubleday, 1992), 109.

2. C. E. B Cranfield, *A Critical and Exegetical Commentary on The Epistle to the Romans* (Edinburgh: Morrison and Gibb, 1975), 441.

3. Ibid., 442.

4. Kent Harold Richards, *The Anchor Bible Dictionary,* ed. David Noel Freedman, vol. 2, D-G (New York: Doubleday, 1992), 110–11.

5. N. Thomas Wright, *The New Interpreter's Bible,* ed. Leander E. Keck, vol. 10, Introduction to Epistolary Literature; Romans; 1 Corinthians (Nashville: Abingdon Press, 2002), 609.

6. Ibid., 613.

7. Ibid., 618.

8. Joseph A. Fitzmyer, *Romans: A New Translation with Introduction and Commentary* (New York: Doubleday, 1993), 536.

9. Ibid., 535.

10. Wright, *The New Interpreter's Bible,* 619.

11. Ibid.

12. Eric Krakauer, Christopher Crenner, and Ken Fox, "Barriers to Optimum End-of-Life Care for Minority Patients," *Journal of the American Geriatric Society* 1, no. 50 (January 2002): 182.

13. Before Medicare, the Hill-Burton Act was the largest federal grant program in health care after World War II. It was entitled the Hospital Survey and Construction Act of 1946, although it was commonly known as the Hill-Burton Act. The Hill-Burton Act was designed to increase the number of hospital beds throughout the country, particularly in rural communities. It sought to provide equal facilities for all citizens, but it allowed hospitals that were receiving federal funds to continue existing patterns of discrimination on the basis of a separate-but-equal provision in the legislation. See P. Preston Reynolds, "Hospitals and Civil Rights, 1945–1963: The Case of *Simkins v. Moses H. Cone Memorial Hospital,*" *Annals of Internal Medicine* 126, no. 11 (June 1997): 901.

14. K. Kahn, M. Pearson, and E. Harrison, "Health-care for Black and Poor Hospitalized Medicare Patients," *Journal of the American Medical Association* no. 271 (1994): 1170.

15. M. Borum, J. Lynn, and Z. Zhong, "The Effects of Patient Race on Outcomes in Seriously Ill Patients in SUPPORT: An Overview of Economic Impact, Medical Intervention, and End-of-life Decisions," *Journal of the American Geriatric Society* 48, no. 5 (2000): S195–96.

16. J. Garrett et al., "Life Sustaining Treatment during Terminal Illness: Who Wants What?" *Journal of Geriatrics in Internal Medicine* no. 8 (1993): 363.

17. P. Caralis et al., "The Influence of Ethnicity and Race on Attitudes Towards Advance Directives, Life-Prolonging Treatments, and Euthanasia," *Journal of Clinical Ethics* no. 4 (1993): 157, 165.

18. Sean R. Morrison and Diane E. Meier, "High Rates of Advance Care Planning in New York City's Elderly Population," *Archives of Internal Medicine* 164 (December 13/27, 2004): 2425.

19. Wendi Born et al., "Knowledge, Attitudes, and Beliefs about End-of-life Care among Inner-City African Americans and Latinos," *Journal of Palliative Medicine* 7, no. 2 (2004): 250.

20. Ibid.

21. Ibid., 251.

22. Ibid.

23. Ibid.

24. DeSpelder and Strickland, *The Last Dance,* 152–53.

25. An excellent new resource can be found at *www.healthcarechaplaincy.org/ userimages/CulturalSpiritualSensitivityLearning/%20Module%207-10-09.pdf.*

26. James Cone, *A Black Theology of Liberation* (Maryknoll, N.Y.: Orbis Books, 1990), 80.

Chapter 5: Our Own Demons

1. See chapter 7 for adapting this for congregational use.

Chapter 6: Preparing for the End of Life

1. These studies include: S. M. Holmes, M. W. Rabow, S. L. Dibble, "Screening the Soul: Communication Regarding Spiritual Concerns among Primary Care Physicians and Seriously Ill Patients Approaching the End of Life," *American Journal of Hospice and Palliative Medicine* 23, no. 1 (January–February 2006): 25–31; D. B. Hinshaw, "Spiritual Issues in Surgical Palliative Care," *Surgical Clinics of North America* 85, no. 2 (1999): 257–72; K. E. Steinhauser et al., "In Search of a Good Death: Observations of Patients, Families and Providers," *Annals of Internal Medicine* 132, no. 10 (May 16, 2000): 825–32.

2. Gallup Institute, 34–35.

3. Martha R. Jacobs, "Opening Up to Atonement," *Living Pulpit* 16, no. 2 (April–June 2007): 20–21.

4. Edwin R. DuBose, "Spiritual Care at the End of Life," *Second Opinion,* Park Ridge Center, no. 10 (April 2002): 39.

5. Ibid., 40.

6. Susan K. Wintz, "Being Mindful of Our Words," *PlainViews* 4, no. 11 (July 5, 2007).

7. DuBose, "Spiritual Care at the End of Life," 53.

Chapter 7: Working with Congregations

1. Pew Research Center, 11.

2. Gallup Institute, 26.

3. Ibid., 1.

4. DeBose, "Spiritual Care at the End of Life," 65.

5. Andrew Lustig, "End-of-life Decisions: Does Faith Make a Difference?" Ethics Watch, *Commonweal,* May 23, 2003.

6. Compassion Sabbath Resource Kit, Center for Practical Bioethics, 1999, Sec. 1, 11.

7. DeBose, "Spiritual Care at the End of Life,"65.

8. Harry Zorn, "Theological Insights into the Role of the Clergy in the Care of the Terminally Ill," *Trends in Health Care, Law, and Ethics* 9, no. 2 (Spring 1994): 30.

9. EndLink: An Internet-based end of life care education program, *http://endlink .lurie.northwestern.edu/more_about/communities.cfm.*

10. Kathryn L. Braun and Reiko Kayashima, "Death Education in Churches and Temples: Engaging Religious Leaders in the Development of Educational Strategies," in *End of Life Issues: Interdisciplinary and Multidisciplinary Perspectives,* ed. Brian deVries, Springer Series on Death and Suicide (New York: Springer Publishing, 1999), 327.

11. *Choices and Conversations: A Guide to End of Life Care for Rhode Island Families* (November 2000): 12.

12. Joseph J. Fins, "Commentary: From Contract to Covenant in Advance Care Planning," *Journal of Law, Medicine, and Ethics* 27 (1999): 46–51.

13. W. A. Ewell, ed., *Baker Encyclopedia of the Bible,* vol. 1 (Grand Rapids: Baker Book House, 1998), 531.

14. Shelly A. Lee, "Voice," *Journal of Financial Planning* (July 2005): 13.

15. Ibid., 12.

16. Pew Research Center, 14.

Chapter 8: Knowing the Options

1. Harry Zorn, "Theological Insights into the Role of the Clergy in the Care of the Terminally Ill," 32.

2. Compassion Sabbath Resource Kit, Center for Practical Bioethics, 1999.

3. "Means to a Better End: A Report on Dying in America Today." See online *www.rwjf.org/pr/product.jsp?id=15799,* November 2002.

4. Kleespies, *Life and Death Decisions,* 143–44.

5. Joanne Lynn, "Living Long in Fragile Health: The New Demographics Share End of Life Care," *Improving End of Life Care: Why Has It Been so Difficult? Hastings Center Report Special Report* 35, no. 6 (2005): S15.

6. *www.ncbi,nlm.nih.gov/pmc/articles/PMC1282187/,* accessed December 17, 2009.

7. World Health Organization, 2007. "Programs and Projects: Cancer and Palliative Care," from *www.who.int/cancer/palliative/en/.*

8. "Task Force on Palliative Care, Last Acts," *Precepts of Palliative Care* (December 1997). *www.aacn.org/WD/Palliative/Docs/2001Precep.pdf,* accessed February 9, 2009.

9. Joanne Lynn is an internationally known leader in helping terminally ill patients improve quality of life.

10. Joanne Lynn, David M. Adamson, "Living Well at the End of Life: Adapting Health Care to Serious Chronic Illness in Old Age," *RAND* (2003): 10.

11. U.S. Government Health and Human Services website: *www.medicare.gov/LongTermCare/static/Home.asp,* accessed February 9, 2009.

12. Ibid.

13. Ibid.

Chapter 9: Focusing on Transformation

1. Personal e-mail exchange with the Rev. Stephen Harding, BCC, February 23, 2009.

2. Personal e-mail exchange with Chaplain Jane Mather, BCC, February 23, 2009.

3. Personal e-mail exchange with the Rev. Dr. Sarah Fogg, BCC, February 24, 2009.

4. Personal e-mail exchange with the Rev. Jill Bowden, BCC, February 23, 2009.

5. *A Greek Lexicon of the New Testament and Other Early Christian Literature,* 3rd ed., s.v. "metanoia."

6. James Forsyth, *Faith and Human Transformation: A Dialogue between Psychology and Theology* (Lanham, Md.: University Press of America, 1997), 126.

Bibliography

Journal Articles

Born, Wendi, et al. "Knowledge, Attitudes, and Beliefs about End-of-life Care among Inner-City African Americans and Latinos." *Journal of Palliative Medicine* 7, no. 2 (2004): 247–56.

Borum, M., J. Lynn, and Z. Zhong. "The Effects of Patient Race on Outcomes in Seriously Ill Patients in SUPPORT: An Overview of Economic Impact, Medical Intervention, and End-of-life Decisions." *Journal of the American Geriatric Society* 48 (2000): S195–96.

Callahan, Daniel. "Death, Mourning and Medical Progress." *Perspectives in Biology and Medicine* 52, no. 1 (Winter 2009): 103–15.

Caralis, P. V., et al. "The Influence of Ethnicity and Race on Attitudes towards Advance Directives, Life-Prolonging Treatments, and Euthanasia." *Journal of Clinical Ethics* 4, no. 2 (Summer 1993): 155–65.

Cook, Deborah, et al. "Withdrawal of Mechanical Ventilation in Anticipation of Death in the Intensive Care Unit." *New England Journal of Medicine* 349, no. 12 (September 18, 2003): 1123–32.

Fagerlin, Angela, and Carl E. Schneider. "Enough: The Failure of the Living Will." *Hastings Center Report* 34, no. 2 (March–April 2004): 30–42.

Fins, Joseph J. "Commentary: From Contract to Covenant in Advance Care Planning." *Journal of Law, Medicine, and Ethics* 27 (1999): 46–51.

Garrett, J., et al. "Life Sustaining Treatment During Terminal Illness: Who Wants What?" *Journal of Geriatrics in Internal Medicine* 8 (1993): 361–68.

Gostin, Lawrence O. "Deciding Life and Death in the Courtroom: From Quinlan to Cruzan, Glucksberg and Vacco — a Brief History and Analysis of Constitutional Protection of the 'Right to Die.'" *Journal of the American Medical Association* 278, no. 18 (November 12, 1997): 1523–28.

Hinshaw, D. B. "Spiritual Issues in Surgical Palliative Care." *Surgical Clinics of North America* 85, no. 2 (1995): 257–72.

Holmes, S. M., M. W. Rabow, and S. L. Dibble. "Screening the Soul: Communication Regarding Spiritual Concerns among Primary Care Physicians and Seriously Ill Patients Approaching the End of Life." *American Journal of Hospice and Palliative Medicine* 23, no. 1 (January/February 2006): 25–31.

Kahn, K., M. Pearson, and E. Harrison. "Health Care for Black and Poor Hospitalized Medicare Patients." *Journal of the American Medical Association* 271 (1994): 1169–74.

161

Krakauer, Eric L., Christopher Crenner, and Ken Fox. "Barriers to Optimum End-of-life Care for Minority Patients." *Journal of the American Geriatrics Society* 50, no. 1 (January 2002): 182–90.

Luce, J., and A. Alpers. "End-of-life Care: What Do American Courts Say?" *Critical Care Medicine* 29, no. 2 Suppl (2001): N40–N45.

Lynn, Joanne. "Living Long in Fragile Health: The New Demographics Share End of Life Care; Improving End of life Care: Why Has It Been so Difficult?" *Hastings Center Report Special Report* 35, no. 6 (2005), S14–18.

Morrison, Sean R., and Diane E. Meier. "High Rates of Advance Care Planning in New York City's Elderly Population." *Archives of Internal Medicine* 164 (December 13–17, 2004): 2421–26.

Murray, Thomas H., and Bruce Jennings. "The Quest to Reform End of Life Care: Rethinking Assumptions and Setting New Directions." *Hastings Center Report Special Report* 35, no. 6 (2005): S56.

Reynolds, P. Preston. "Hospitals and Civil Rights: 1945–1963 — the Case of Simpkins v. Moses H. Cone Memorial Hospital." *Annals of Internal Medicine* 126, no. 11 (June 1, 1997): 898–906.

Steinhauser, K. E. et al. "Factors Considered Important at the End of Life by Patients, Family, Physicians and Other Care Providers." *Journal of the American Medical Association* 284, no. 19 (November 2000): 2476–82.

———. "In Search of a Good Death: Observations of Patients, Families and Providers" *Annals of Internal Medicine* 132, no. 10 (May 16, 2000): 825–32.

Wilson J. "Health Insurance Portability and Accountability Act Privacy Rule Causes Ongoing Concerns among Clinicians and Researchers." *Annals Intern Medicine* 145, no. 4 (2006): 313–16.

Zorn, Harry. "Theological Insights into the Role of the Clergy in the Care of the Terminally Ill." *Trends in Health Care, Law, and Ethics* 9, no. 2 (Spring 1994).

Books

Becker, Ernest. *The Denial of Death*. New York: Macmillan, 1973.

Braun, Kathryn L. and Reiko Kayashima. "Death Education in Churches and Temples: Engaging Religious Leaders in the Development of Educational Strategies." *In End of Life Issues: Interdisciplinary and Multidisciplinary Perspectives*. Ed. Brian deVries. Springer Series on Death and Suicide. New York: Springer Publishing, 1999.

Coffin, William Sloane. *Credo*. Louisville: Westminster John Knox Press, 2004.

Cone, James. *A Black Theology of Liberation*. New York: Orbis Books, 1990.

Cranfield, C. E. B. *A Critical and Exegetical Commentary on The Epistle to the Romans*. Edinburgh: Morrison and Gibb, 1975.

DeSpelder, Lynne Ann, and Albert Lee Strickland. *The Last Dance: Encountering Death and Dying*. New York: McGraw Hill, 2002.

Ewell, W. A., ed. *Baker Encyclopedia of the Bible*. Vol. 1. Grand Rapids: Baker Book House, 1998.

Fitzmyer, Joseph A. *Romans: A New Translation with Introduction and Commentary*. New York: Doubleday, 1993.

Forsyth, James. *Faith and Human Transformation: A Dialogue between Psychology and Theology.* Lanham, Md.: University Press of America, 1997.

Freedman, David Noel, ed. *The Anchor Bible Dictionary.* New York: Doubleday, 1992.

Hale, W. Daniel, and Harold G. Koenig. *Healing Bodies and Souls — a Practical Guide for Congregations.* Minneapolis: Fortress Press, 2003.

Kleespies, Phillip M. *Life and Death Decisions: Psychological and Ethical Considerations in End-of-Life Care.* Washington, D.C.: American Psychological Association, 2004.

Meeks, Wayne A., ed. *The HarperCollins Study Bible.* New York: HarperCollins, 1989.

Meyer, Charles. *A Good Death: Challenges, Choices and Care Options.* Mystic, Conn.: Twenty-Third Publications, 2000.

Mohrmann, Margaret. *Medicine as Ministry.* Cleveland: Pilgrim Press, 1995.

Richards, Kent Harold. *The Anchor Bible Dictionary.* Ed. David Noel Freedman. Vol. 2, D-G. New York: Doubleday, 1992.

Smith, Paul. *The Deep Calling to the Deep: Facing Death.* Brooklyn Heights, N.Y.: Coat of Many Colors, 1998.

Other Works

Choices and Conversations: A Guide to End of Life Care for Rhode Island Families, November, 2000.

Compassion Sabbath Resource Kit, Center for Practical Bioethics, 1999.

Davis, Dena S. "Old and Thin." *Second Opinion* 15 (November 1990): 26–32.

DuBose, Edwin R. "Spiritual Care at the End of Life." *Second Opinion.* The Park Ridge Center, no. 10 (April 2002): 4–74.

George H. Gallup International Institute. "Spiritual Beliefs and the Dying Process, a Report of a National Survey Conducted for the Nathan Cummings Foundation and Fetzer Institute." Princeton, N.J.: The George H. Gallop International Institute, 1997.

Gross, Jane. "Keeping Patients' Details Private, Even from Kin." *New York Times,* July 3, 2007.

Harley, Julie Ruth, ed. *Making End-of-Life Decisions: United Church of Christ Perspectives 1993.* Cleveland: Council for Health and Human Services Ministries, 1993.

Jacobs, Martha R. "Opening Up to Atonement." *Living Pulpit* 16, no. 2 (April–June 2007): 20–21.

Lee, Shelly A. "Voice." *Journal of Financial Planning* (July 2005): 13.

Lynn, Joanne, and David M. Adamson. "Living Well at the End of Life: Adapting Health Care to Serious Chronic Illness in Old Age." *RAND* (2003): 10.

Lustig, Andrew. "End-of-life Decisions: Does Faith Make a Difference?" *Ethics Watch, Commonweal,* May 23, 2003.

"Means to a Better End: A Report on Dying in America Today," *www.rwjf.org/pr/product.jsp?id=15788.* November 2002.

Midwest Bioethics Centers, press release. "Pastors, Rabbis, Priests Often Unprepared to Address Spiritual Needs of the Dying: Faith Leaders Flock to Ministering-to-the-Dying Summit February 2–4 — Kansas City" (press release dated January 18, 2001).

Pew Research Center for the People and the Press. "More Americans Discussing — and Planning — End-of-Life Treatment: Strong Public Support for Right to Die," January 5, 2006.

Schloendorff v. Society of New York Hospital, 211 NY 125, 105 NE 92 (1914).

Spafford, Horatio, "It is Well with My Soul," 1873.

Union Pacific Railway Co v. Botsford, 141 US 250, 251 (1891).

Wintz, Susan K. "Being Mindful of Our Words." *PlainViews* 4, no. 11 (July 5, 2007).

Websites

Center for Bioethics, University of Minnesota.
www.ahc.umn.edu/img/assets/26104/End_of_Life.pdf.

Centers for Medicare and Medicaid Services.
www.cms.hhs.gov/HIPAAGenInfo/02_TheHIPAALawandRelated%20 Information.asp#TopOfPage.

Medicinenet.com.
www.medicinenet.com/congestive_heart_failure/article.htm.

Merck Manuals Online Medical Library.
www.merck.com/mmpe/sec16/ch212/ch212d.html.

New York State Department of Health website.
www.health.state.ny.us/professionals/patients/patient_rights/most/frequently _asked_questions.htm.

Physician Orders for Life-Sustaining Treatment (POLST) Paradigm.
www.ohsu.edu/ethics/polst/.

Task Force on Palliative Care.
www.aacn.org/WD/Palliative/Docs/2001Precep.pdf.

University of Buffalo Center for Clinical Ethics and Humanities in Health Care.
http://wings.buffalo.edu/bioethics/oconnor1.html.

U.S. Government Health and Human Services website.
www.medicare.gov/LongTermCare/static/Home.asp.

World Health Organization.
www.who.int/cancer/palliative/en/.